A MATTER OF TASTE

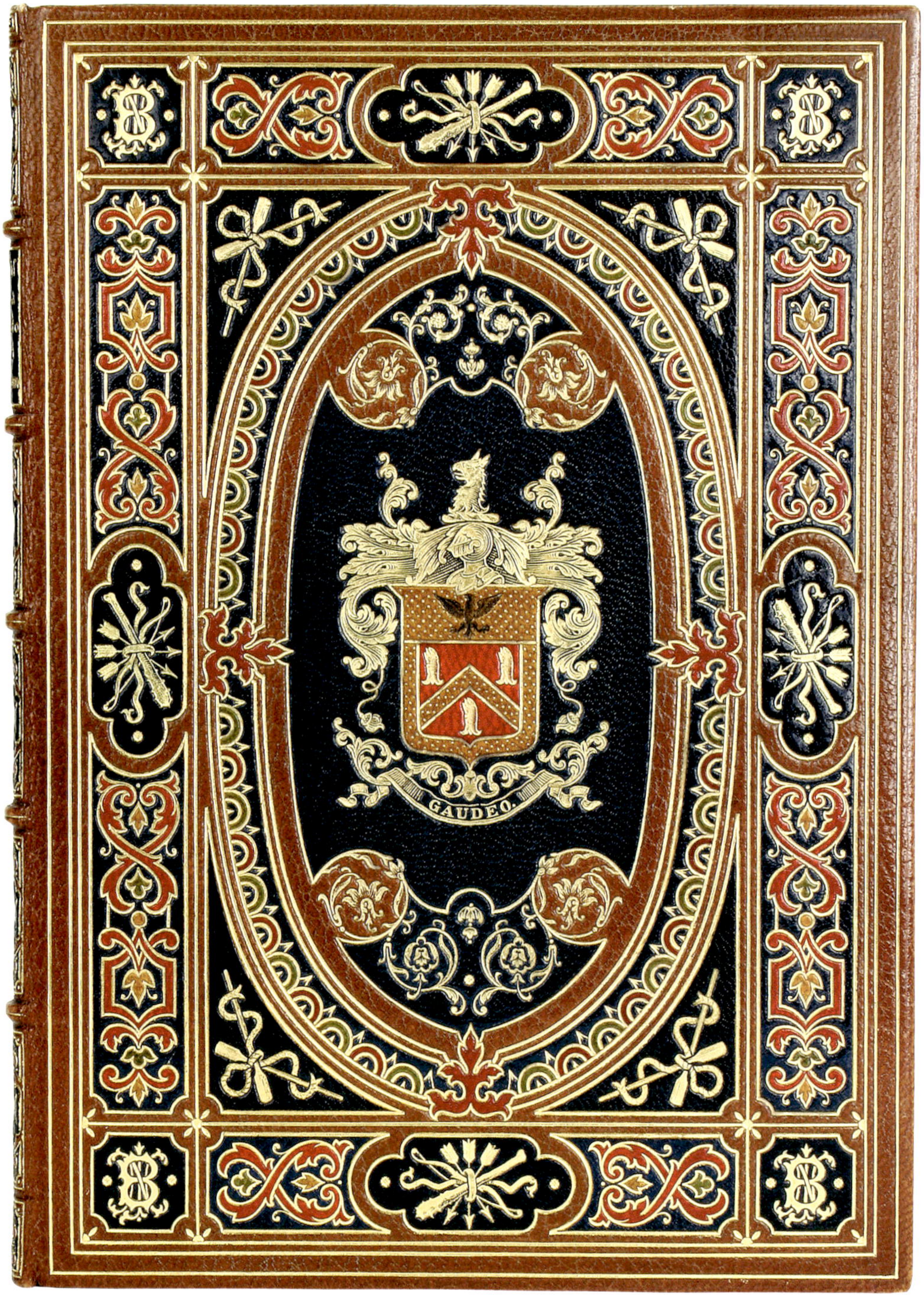
GAUDEO.

A MATTER OF TASTE

Discrimination in Nineteenth-Century Book Collecting

*Catalogue of an Exhibition of Rare Books
from the John Carter Brown Library*

Susan Danforth

Photographs by Richard Hurley

Published for the Associates of

THE JOHN CARTER BROWN LIBRARY

Providence, Rhode Island

MMVIII

FRONTISPIECE: Columbus *Epistola* (1493), bound for John Nicholas Brown by F. Cuzin.

Photographs by Richard Hurley, with the assistance of John Carter Brown digital imaging staff.

Copyright 2008 by the John Carter Brown Library
All rights reserved

This work may not be reproduced in part or whole, in any form or medium, for any purpose, without permission in writing from the copyright owner.

The John Carter Brown Library is an independently funded and administered institution for advanced research in history and the humanities, located at Brown University since 1901. The Library houses one of the world's outstanding collections of books, maps, and manuscripts relating to the colonial period of the Americas, North and South, from 1493 to ca. 1825.

Correspondence should be directed to the
John Carter Brown Library
Box 1894
Providence, Rhode Island 02912
or to
JCBL_Publications@brown.edu
Additional information may be found at *www.jcbl.org*

ISBN 0-916617-67-x

Contents

List of Illustrations vii

Foreword by Dr. Philip Maddock xi

Preface by Ted Widmer xv

Introduction by Susan Danforth xix

PART I
Identification   2

    BOOK BRANDS
    INK STAMPS
    BINDING STAMPS
    BOOKPLATES

PART II
Binding 16

    BINDING IN THE FRENCH STYLE
    BINDING IN THE ENGLISH STYLE
    SEVENTEENTH-CENTURY AMERICAN BINDING
    FIFTEENTH-CENTURY GERMAN BINDING
    CHAINED BINDING
    "IT IS, AFTER ALL, A MATTER OF TASTE"

PART III
Restoration 33

    PEN AND INK FACSIMILES
        Title Page
        Missing Leaves
    PAPER REPAIR
    "TRADING UP"
    SOPHISTICATION
        Tall and Short
        Sophistication Incomplete
        More Is More
    "I THINK IT BEST NOT TO TAMPER WITH IT"

PART IV
Replication 53
    PEN AND INK FACSIMILES
        Columbus Letters
        John Harris, Facsimile Artist
    THE USUAL SITUATION, REVERSED

PART V
Collecting the Voyages *of Theodor de Bry* 64
    LARGE AND SMALL
    "ENDLESS" VARIATION
    THE DISCUSSION CONTINUES
    "IT WOULD STILL BE BUT AN IMITATION"
    WASHING AND DRY CLEANING

PART VI
Collecting the Aldine Press 76
    MAKE HASTE SLOWLY
    CREATIVE COUNTERFEITS

PART VII
Fore-Edge Painting 84

List of Illustrations

Frontispiece

PART I

Identification

   I.1 Selection of book brands from Mexican libraries.
   I.2 Selection of John Carter Brown's ink stamps.
   I.3 Ink stamp on *A relation of the invasion and conquest of Florida* (1686).
   I.4 Ink stamp on title page of Cortés, *Praeclara* (1524).
   I.5 Binding dies of Henri Ternaux-Compans and John Carter Brown.
   I.6 John Carter Brown's large initial binding die.
   I.7 John Carter Brown's coat-of-arms binding die.
   I.8 Bookplates of John Percival, Earl of Egmont, and Dr. Nicolás León.
   I.9 Dr. Nicolás León in his library.
   I.10 Selection of John Carter Brown Library book plates.

PART II

Binding

   II.1 Binders' tools used for the decoration of Columbus letters.
   II.2 Columbus *Letter,* bound by F. Cuzin.
   II.3 Columbus *Letter* (1493), bound by F. Cuzin.
   II.4 Whitbourne, *Discourse* (1620), bound by Chambolle-Duru.
   II.5 Steendam, *Nuw-Nederland* (1661), bound by Chambolle-Duru.
   II.6 Roger Payne (1739–1797).
   II.7 González de Mendoza, *Historie* (1589), bound by Francis Bedford.
   II.8 *Bay Psalm Book* (1640), bound by John Ratcliff (fl. 1651–1682).
   II.9 Ptolemy, *Geography* (1482), with original boards and pigskin binding.
   II.10 Jewell, *Works* (1609), with chained binding.
   II.11 Bocaccio, *La ruine des nobles hommes…* (1476), bound by F. Cuzin.
   II.12 Invoice: F. Cuzin to John Nicholas Brown (October 18, 1887).

PART III

Restoration

    III.1 Invoice: Francis Bedford to the Estate of John Carter Brown (May 10, 1875).

    III.2 Facsimile title page, Cortés, *Breve compendio* (1551).

    III.3 Facsimile of Nuñez Cabeza de Vaca, *La relacion* (1542).

    III.4 Invoice: Francis Bedford to Sophia Augusta Brown (October 13, 1879).

    III.5 Repaired title page, Increase Mather, *The right way to shake off a viper* (1720).

    III.6 Repaired title page, Increase Mather, *Wo to drunkards* (1712).

    III.7 Title page of *Virginia richly valued* (1609).

    III.8 Spain, *Leyes y ordenancas* (1543), showing paper repairs.

    III.9 Imperfect copies of *Huehuetlahtolli* (1601).

    III.10 Thévenot's *Relations* (1663), showing two of the four variant title pages.

    III.11 Smith's *True travels* (1630), with binding from the library of Charles II.

PART IV

Replication

    IV.1 Title page of Settle, A *true report of the late voyage…* (1577).

    IV.2 Facsimile edition of Settle, A *true report of the late voyage…*, printed for John Carter Brown in 1868.

    IV.3 Columbus, *Epistola* (1493).

    IV.4 Facsimile of Columbus, *Epistola* (1493).

    IV.5 John Harris's pen and ink facsimile in Humphrey Gilbert, *Discourse* (1576).

    IV.6 Columbus, *Epistola* (1497)

    IV.7 Facsimile of Columbus, *Epistola* (1497).

    IV.8 Vespucci, *Von der neu gefunden Region* (1505).

PART V

Collecting the Voyages *of Theodor de Bry*

    V.1 Size comparison of de Bry's "Grands" and "Petits" voyages.

    V.2 Upside down illustration in de Bry's *Grands voyages*. Part 3 (1592).

    V.3 Title page of the first edition of de Bry's *Grands voyages*, Part 2 (1591).

    V.4 de Bry's *Grands voyages*, Part 4 (1594), showing inserted engraving.

    V.5 Invoice: Francis Bedford to Messrs. Rimell & Son (for John Carter Brown) (August 23, 1874).

    V.6 Alligator hunt from de Bry with washed paper.

    V.7 Alligator hunt from de Bry with dry-cleaned paper.

PART VI
Collecting the Aldine Press
    VI.1   Selection of books from the Aldine Press.
    VI.2   Dolphin and anchor on title page of Ricchieri, *Sciuti antiquarum* (1516).
    VI.3   Title page of the counterfeit edition, Portio, *La congiura* (1565?).
    VI.4   Entry for Portio's *La congiura* (1565?) in John Carter Brown's "Catalogue of Aldine Editions" (1862).

PART VII
Fore-Edge Painting
    VII.1   Seascape on the fore-edge of *The whole book of psalms* (1798).
    VII.2   Seascape on the fore-edge of Wilberforce, *A practical view* (1829).

Foreword

It is with great pleasure that I introduce Susan Danforth's study of John Carter Brown (d. 1874) and his son, John Nicholas (d. 1900), as collectors. Several years ago, Philip Weimerskirch of the Providence Public Library told me about an interesting exhibition at the John Carter Brown Library. After my first visit I realized how important and informative the exhibition was, and I returned for many further hours of study. Ms. Danforth's emphasis is on the collector and collecting rather than on the collection, with additional attention paid to collecting techniques and related issues of the late nineteenth century. Traditional bookbinding in late-nineteenth-century Britain attained one of its climaxes and this exhibition captures the moment.

As a book collector myself I find it quite heartening that both John Carter Brown and John Nicholas Brown faced many of the temptations and quandaries that continue to bedevil book collectors in putting together a library that satisfies the collecting urge while respecting the integrity of the books themselves. When is one justified in combining parts of two or three incomplete books to make one whole book? Merely stating the question raises the problem of what constitutes a "whole book" bibliographically.

Ms. Danforth also draws attention to the art/practice of the pen facsimile, a more extreme method of fixing a defective book. At a bookbinding conference I once attended, there was a collective gasp from the audience when an expert demonstrated how a pen facsimile is done. In the Q & A session afterwards, one of the more forward postgraduate students practically accused him of forgery. One wonders in these days of easily acquired scans and photocopies how the artisans gained access to the originals from which they copied their pen facsimiles. Ms. Danforth places such practices, quite common in the period of this exhibition, in context, elucidating the thinking and tastes of the discriminating collector of that era.

The exhibition also makes clear the importance of the relationship between the bookseller and the collector in terms of mutual education. On page 30 there is a letter from Frank Ellis to John Nicholas Brown, July 20, 1886, recommending minimum restoration to a 1476 book. In the event, Brown instead sent the book to Paris where it was rebound by Cuzin in black Morocco. By 1893, however, John Nicholas Brown had progressed to the point where he refused Henry N. Stevens's offer to sophisticate a copy of Capt. John Smith's *True Travels*. The exhibition and this resulting catalogue are an inspiration to all collectors and book lovers to do better.

The Browns were indeed fortunate in the friends and acquaintances they made in the book collecting world. This exhibition has inspired me to research Bartlett, Stevens, Ellis, and Bedford the London binder. The Browns were even luckier in their librarians and one thinks especially of George Parker Winship and Lawrence C.

Wroth. It has been my good fortune to know the recently retired librarian Norman Fiering for many years. I had originally hoped that this book would be ready as a mark of respect on his official day of retiring. Fortunately, he continues as emeritus librarian. Thank you, Norman. As they say in Ireland, *better late than never*.

—Philip G. Maddock, MD, MA.
Barrington, Rhode Island

Preface

M<small>OST OF THE PATRONS</small> of the John Carter Brown Library come to Providence, in some cases from great distances, to discover what lies *within* our books. This publication, the result of a stunning exhibition curated by Susan Danforth, takes a very different approach. By treating the book as a beautiful object, and its external appearance in particular, it allows the reader to consider the face that each of these singular creations presents to the outside world.

Well before we open a book, we have encountered it in numerous ways, responding to the binding, shape, and overall feel of an artisanal product that is not nearly as distant as we might imagine from the shop where it was brought to life. And I do mean life—Susan tells me that the books of the JCB expand and contract with the weather, and even fight each other for space on the shelves, sometimes knocking themselves onto the floor from the effort. For all the erudition represented in this collection, we must never forget that these remarkable artifacts were assembled from cows, pigs, and trees before acquiring their sophistication. They are alive in every sense.

In many profound ways this work is a celebration of the JCB's heritage. It draws upon the expertise of a curator who has cared for these books for 33 years and counting. Its publication was made possible by a loyal Associate who was moved by the exhibit, and wanted to perpetuate it for his fellow Associates. And it honors the extraordinary bibliophilia of a family that has nurtured this still-growing collection for two centuries and more. Indeed, our earliest book about the New World with a Brown family signature (Samuel Sewall's *Phaenomena quaedam Apocalyptica*) was purchased by Nicholas Brown in 1769. At long last, the JCB has become as venerable as its treasures.

This heritage is eminently worth commemorating, even as we adapt to new readers and new centuries. The digital age may be upon us, and information communicated through a never-ending crackle of electronic announcements, emanating from billboards, laptops, and handheld devices. But despite these changes, and perhaps even because of them, the book stands firm as an anchor of civilization, a bulwark of permanence, and as we can see in the pages to come, a work of considerable beauty. As Frank Ellis wrote to John Nicholas Brown in 1886, "it is after all a matter of taste."

—TED WIDMER
Beatrice and Julio Mario Santo Domingo
Director and Librarian
John Carter Brown Library

Introduction

The urge to collect, preserve, and share the wealth of experience contained in books has an effect, sometimes subtle, on the physical character of the book itself. Whether a collector of ideas is an individual or an institution, the volumes acquired must be protected, preserved, arranged, and made accessible; in short, they must be considered as objects. Focusing upon acquisitions made in the nineteenth century, this publication provides examples from the John Carter Brown Library of some of the effects that taste and trends in book collecting have had on the book as an object. It will come as no surprise that the volumes most affected are those that aroused collectors' desire for their beauty and rarity.

While in some cases the practices typical of the times—Mexican book brands, ink library stamps on title pages, elaborate bindings—have not affected the integrity of the book as an expression of an idea, in other cases judgment may not be so certain. Nineteenth-century collectors' acceptance of "sophistication," the gathering together of bits and pieces of several copies to make one "complete" volume, is cause for concern to a scholar whose interest lies in textual integrity. The demand for carefully constructed facsimiles to complete imperfect books encouraged the specialized talents of artists and printers, and created a skilled group of craftsmen whose copies could fool the eye of the casual observer and could also, at times, cause consternation in scholars' and collectors' circles. Indeed, it is often a fine line that divides facsimile from forgery. In using "rare books" as primary sources for research, an awareness of past practices can aid today's scholar in assessing historical material.

Necessarily, examples have been grouped into broad categories—identification, embellishment, restoration, and an exploration of some particular challenges presented by facsimiles. Special attention is focused upon the series of books published by Aldus Manutius and Theodor de Bry, volumes that bear the burden of a long history of collectibility. The section on the Aldines points up collection problems posed by this special group of books, which were actively collected as early as the sixteenth century and just as enthusiastically presented to the buying public in forged (or more fairly perhaps, in "pirated" or "unauthorized") editions. The de Bry "Grands" and "Petits" voyages, were an early attempt to present the European public with a narrative and visual overview of events occurring on the fringes of the "civilized" world. Profusely illustrated and bibliographically complex, these books appealed to European collectors of "great books" and linked their traditional approach to the less usual *subject* collecting of men like John Carter Brown. The Library's set of de Bry consists of nearly 100 gold-tooled red morocco volumes uniformly bound by Francis Bedford.

No attempt has been made to be comprehensive, and many of the books shown as examples in one category could just as well illustrate another. This publication has been presented, rather, as food for thought for the advanced collector and the amateur attracted to books as objects and as ideas.

—Susan Danforth
George S. Parker II Curator of Maps

A MATTER OF TASTE

PART I:
Identification

BOOK BRANDS

THE BOOK BRAND is a dramatic statement of ownership commonly found on volumes with Mexican library provenance. Effective permanent identification, a brand could not be reversed. It could be altered and trimmed, but because these Mexican and Spanish books on religious topics were not sought by European and American collectors in the same way as more traditional "beautiful" and "important" books, they were less likely to have been trimmed and gilded by European "society" binders and are often found in this, their original, condition.

TITLES ILLUSTRATED

Antonio de Escobar y Mendoza, *Nueva Jerusalen*, Mexico, 1758. (fig. I.1)

Lope Felix de Vega Carpio, *Triunfo de la fee*, Madrid, 1618. (fig. I.1)

Catholic Church, *Manual de administrar los santos sacramentos*, Mexico, 1638. (fig. I.1)

Angel Serra, *Manual de administrar los santos sacramentos*, Mexico, 1731. (fig. I.1)

1.1
A selection of book brands from Mexican libraries.

INK STAMPS

"What think you of the plan I have before suggested to you of having all my books stamped with my name or initials on the front or back of the fifth pages?"
—John Carter Brown to John Russell Bartlett, November 14, 1848

CONTROVERSY OVER whether or not to stamp the pages of a book with an owner's mark is not new; John Carter Brown was debating the question in 1848. Initially, he mentioned book stamping only for less valuable volumes, but apparently he later became convinced that he should mark most of his collection. It is possible that he considered the red mark a lesser evil than loss or theft. Then, too, if he later decided to dispose of a book, the Brown library provenance could hardly lower its value. Most collectors today would consider the practice defacement.

TITLES ILLUSTRATED

A relation of the invasion and conquest of Florida by the Spaniards, London, 1686. (fig. 1.3)

Hernán Cortés, *Praeclara Ferdina[n]di,* Nuremberg, 1524. (fig. 1.4)

1.2
Selection of John Carter Brown's ink stamps.

1.3
Ink stamp on *A relation of the invasion and conquest of Florida* (1686).

1.4
John Carter Brown's ink stamp on title page of Cortés, *Praeclara* (1524).

BINDING STAMPS

"What would be the cost of stamping books as Ternaux's are done?"
—John Carter Brown to John Russell Bartlett, June 5, 1848.

"The small stamp, of my crest & initials never quite filled my eye—the large ones, the J.C.B. and also the arms—such as are on my Bibles fully meet my views."
—John Carter Brown to John Russell Bartlett, June 5, 1848.

IN THE SELECTION of books for his collection John Carter Brown could not always find volumes in the condition that equaled the standards set by the builders of the great private libraries in Europe, but he did have a concern for the proper presentation of a book as an object. *En bloc* purchases of books from the dispersed library of Henri Ternaux-Compans brought the French collector's characteristic ram's head stamp to Brown's notice and provided an example for the treatment of his own library.

TITLES ILLUSTRATED

Bartolomeu Guerreiro, *Iornada dos vassalos da coroa de Portugal,* Lisbon, 1625, with the stamp of Henri Ternaux-Compans. (fig. 1.5)

Andrew White, *A relation of the successfull beginnings of the Lord Baltemore's plantation in Mary-Land,* [London], 1634, with the stamp of John Carter Brown. (fig. 1.5)

Francisco López de Gómara, *Primera y segunda parte de la historia general de las Indias,* Zaragoza, 1553, with John Carter Brown's large initial binding stamp. (fig. 1.6)

[Willem Usselincx], *Argonautica Gustaviana,* Frankfurt am Mayn, 1633, with John Carter Brown's coat-of-arms stamp. The crest was altered after this binding was stamped. (fig. 1.7)

1.5
Binding stamps of Henri Ternaux-Compans (right) and
John Carter Brown (left). At left, binding die of John Carter Brown.
Heights: 8 inches and 7 inches.

1.6
John Carter Brown's large initial binding die.

1.7
John Carter Brown's coat-of-arms binding die on *Argonautica*.

BOOKPLATES

Collectors typically expend great effort on the design and execution of bookplates to grace the inside covers of their books, both as a decorative mark of possession and as insurance that borrowed volumes will eventually find their way home again. Bookplates sometimes make it possible to follow the path of ownership from collection to collection, and this record is an integral part of the history of the book as an object and as an idea. Often, provenance as demonstrated by previous ownership is the most trustworthy proof that a work is not a counterfeit.

TITLES ILLUSTRATED

William Stephens, *A journal of the proceedings in Georgia,* London, 1742, with bookplates of John Percival, Earl of Egmont (1633–1748), trustee of the colony of Georgia, and John Carter Brown. (fig. 1.8)

Martín de León, *Camino del cielo en lengua Mexicana*, Mexico, 1611, with bookplate of Dr. Nicolás León, from whom John Nicolas Brown purchased many early Mexican imprints. (fig. 1.8)

1.8
Bookplates of John Percival, Earl of Egmont, John Carter Brown and Dr. Nicolás León.
Heights: 8 inches.

1.9
Dr. Nicolás León in his library.

1.10

A selection of John Carter Brown Library book plates.

PART II:
Binding

"I received a few days since your letter of May 18th and today found at the banker's the precious little Dutch tract, Steendam's 'New Netherlands.' This I shall forthwith take to the man recommended by Mr. Ellis as the best binder in Paris and let him repair it and put it into one of his finest bindings—morocco, of course."
—John Nicholas Brown to John Russell Bartlett, June 4, 1883

BINDING IN THE FRENCH STYLE

Bindings, of course, serve purposes other than owner identification. A rare, long-sought-after book often was treated as an elusive prize which, when secured, should be decorated as befitted its station. Whether or not one shares nineteenth-century aesthetic taste, it is always possible to appreciate the skill, artistry, and effort that produced these superb bindings.

TITLES ILLUSTRATED

Christopher Columbus, *Epistola de insulis nuper inventis*, Rome, after 29 April 1493. (fig. II.2)

Christopher Columbus, *Epistola de insulis nuper inventis*, Basel, after 29 April 1493. (fig. II.3)

Richard Whitbourne, *A discourse and discovery of New-Found-Land*, London, 1620. (fig. II.4)

Jacob Steendam, *'T lof van Nuw-Nederland*, Amsterdam, 1661. (fig. II.5)

II.1
Binders' tools used for the decoration of the John Carter Brown Library Columbus letters.

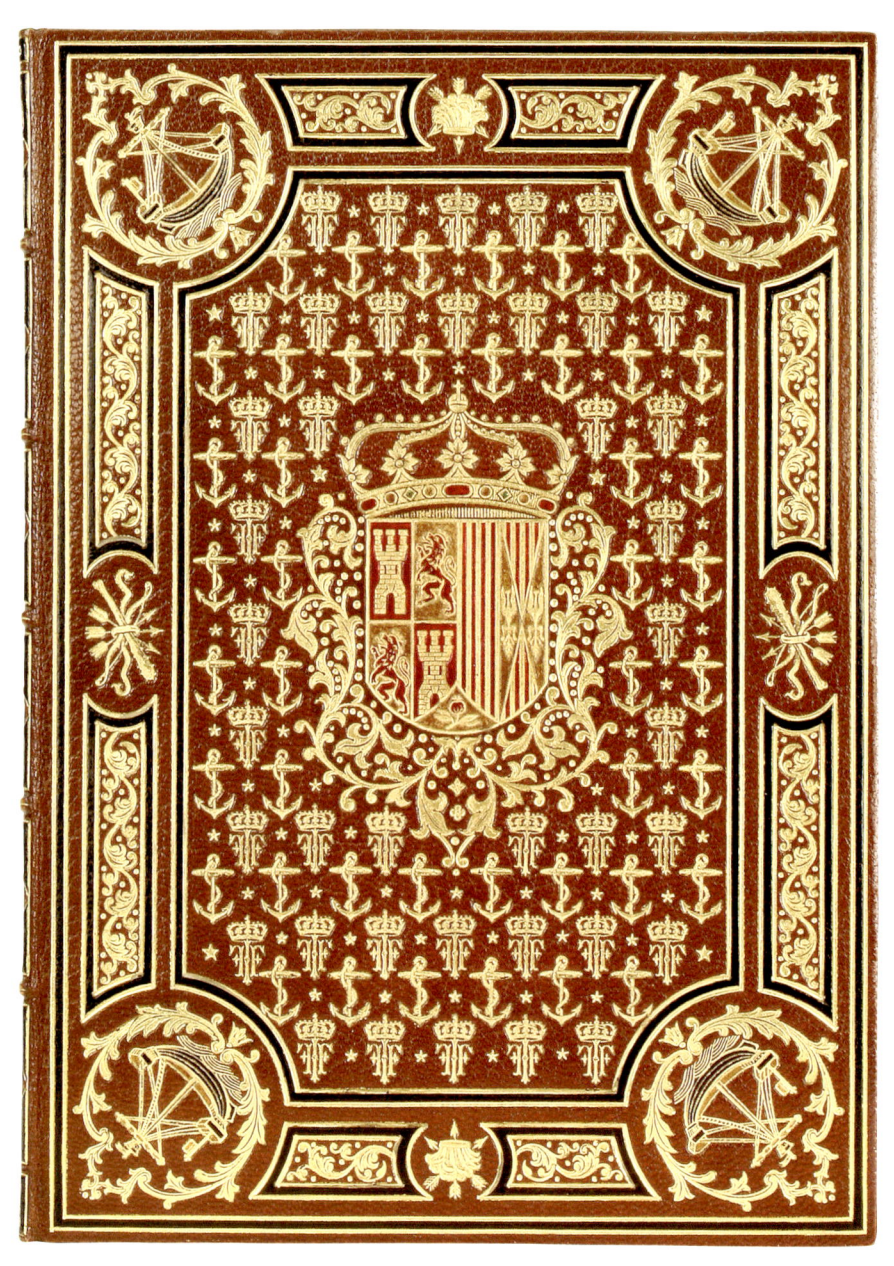

II.2
Columbus *Epistola* (1493), bound for John Nicholas Brown by F. Cuzin.
Height: 7.75 inches.

II.3
Columbus *Epistola* (1493), bound for John Nicholas Brown by F. Cuzin.
Height: 7.25 inches.

II.4
Whitbourne, *Discourse* (1620), bound for John Nicholas Brown by Chambolle-Duru.
Height: 7.25 inches.

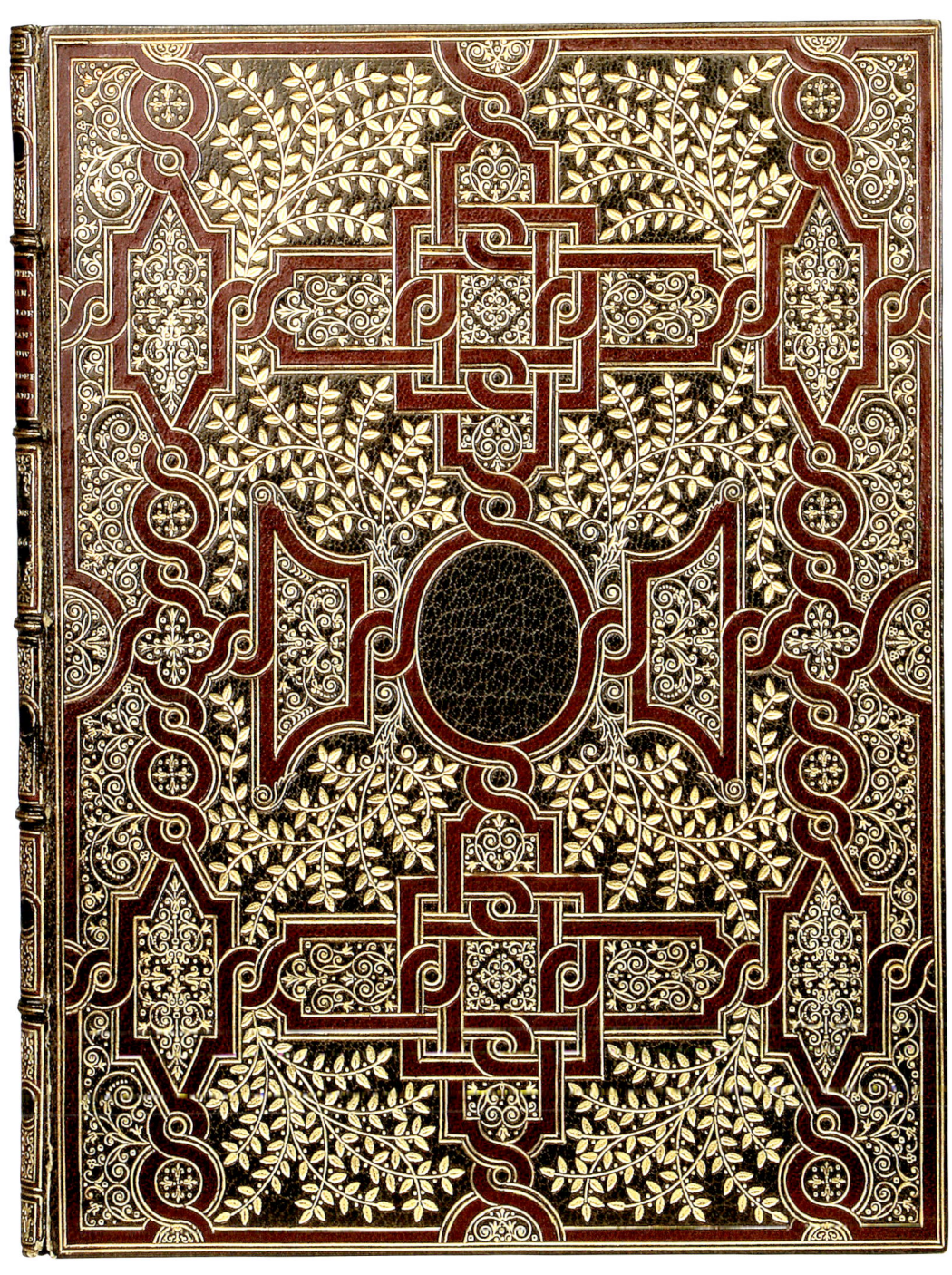

ii.5
Steendam, *Nuw-Nederland* (1661), bound for John Nicholas Brown by Chambolle-Duru.
Height: 8 inches.

BINDING IN THE ENGLISH STYLE

"I have secured a copy of the long-looked for English Mendoca. Ellis had a copy and a fine one too—only a few leaves at the end being soiled. I bought it and left it with him to have bound in red morocco by Bedford, in his Roger Payne style."

—John Nicholas Brown to John Russell Bartlett, May 24, 1883

R‍OGER PAYNE is considered to be the first binder to establish a truly English style of binding. John Nicholas Brown's request to have his "English Mendoca" bound in Bedford's "Roger Payne style" may well have been an early effort to have a book bound appropriately, according to its place of publication, rather than sumptuously, according to its rarity.

TITLE ILLUSTRATED

Juan González de Mendoza, *The historie of the great and mightie kingdome of China,* London, 1588 [i.e. 1589]. (fig. II.7)

11.6
Roger Payne (1739–1797). First published by S. Harding, Pall Mall, London, March 1800.
Copied from Penelope Holt's *Roger Payne, book binder*, 1969.

II.7
González de Mendoza, *Historie* (1589), bound for John Nicholas Brown by Francis Bedford.
Height: 7.5 inches.

II.7
Detail (actual size)

SEVENTEENTH-CENTURY BOSTON BINDING

"I am pleased to be able to tell you that I have got back the Psalm book from Paris admirably got up so that I think you and Mr. John cannot fail to be pleased with it. It looks now as it must have done when a pilgrim father first carried it to meeting with him, barring perhaps the water stains inside, but to have taken those all out would have destroyed the character of the book."

—Frank Ellis to Sophia Augusta Brown, June 20, 1883

THE BAY PSALM BOOK owned by the John Carter Brown Library is a great rarity. It is the only perfect copy still in its original binding and the only copy containing the signature of one of the translators, Richard Mather. The Psalm Book almost received an elaborate new binding at the hands of the "society binder" Francis Bedford, which would have obliterated this singular heritage. Bedford fell ill, however, and John Nicholas Brown chose not to risk leaving the book in Bedford's London shop. Instead, he entrusted the book to the dealer Frank Ellis, who agreed to oversee its repair. Ellis's comment in a letter to Sophia Augusta Brown is an early example of a growing inclination to preserve a volume in its original condition—a desire to respect the "character" of a book.

TITLE ILLUSTRATED

The whole book of psalmes faithfully translated into English metre, [Cambridge, Massachusetts], 1640. (fig. II.8)

II.8
Bay Psalm Book (1640), bound by John Ratcliff (fl. 1651–1682).
Height: 7 inches.

FIFTEENTH-CENTURY GERMAN BINDING

THE FIFTEENTH- and sixteenth-century editions of Ptolemy's *Cosmographia* were extremely popular acquisitions for nineteenth-century collectors who were prone to re-bind them expensively according to the taste of the day. The JCB is fortunate to have this very rare example of a fifteenth-century edition of Ptolemy in its original binding.

TITLE ILLUSTRATED

Claudius Ptolemy, *Cosmographia*, Ulm, 1482. (fig. II.9)

CHAINED BINDING

A RECENT GIFT to the Library is this example of a chained binding. Books were secured by chains—often to a horizontal bar above the reading desk or shelf—in monastic and other libraries from the fifteenth to the early eighteenth centuries.

TITLE ILLUSTRATED

John Jewell, *The works*, London, 1609. Gift of Robert and Ann Robinson. (fig. II.10)

II.9
Ptolemy, *Geography* (1482), with original boards and pigskin binding.
Height: 17 inches.

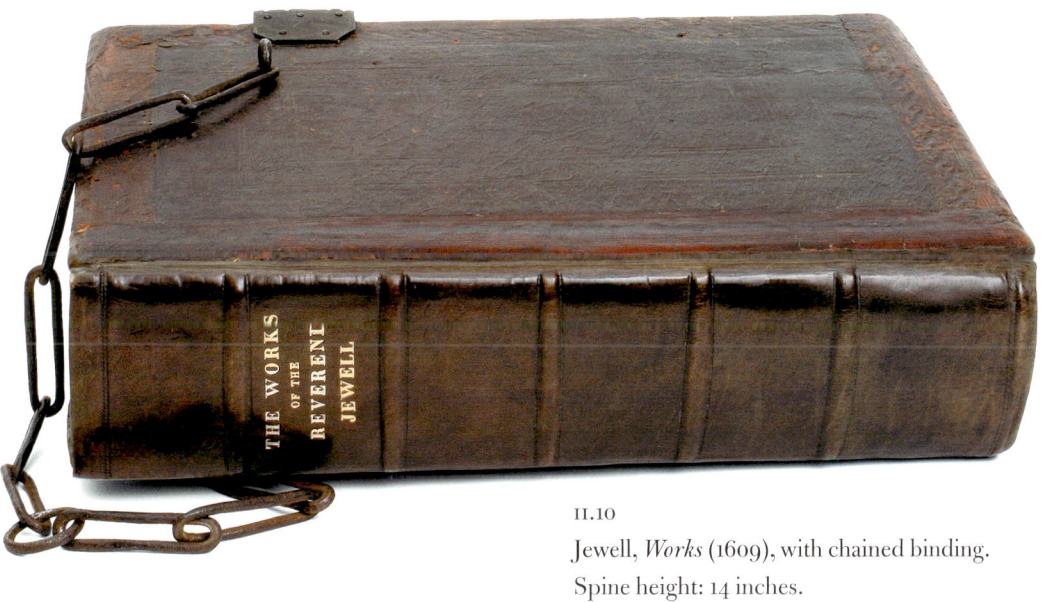

II.10
Jewell, *Works* (1609), with chained binding.
Spine height: 14 inches.

"IT IS, AFTER ALL, A MATTER OF TASTE"

"The condition of the paper is that in which it issued from the hands of poor Colard Mansion and in its present condition you have the advantage—a very great one to the bibliographer—of seeing the strings of the binding & being able to see how the sheets were made up.... When once this volume has passed through the hands of the washer, "restorer," and binder, it will be to a certain extent sophisticated—I should keep it as it is—but as I began by saying, it is after all a matter of taste."

—Frank Ellis to John Nicholas Brown, July 20, 1886

In May 1886, John Nicholas Brown bought this copy of Boccaccio's *La ruine des nobles hommes et femmes*, an example of fine printing from the press of Colard Mansion. When purchased, the book was bound in vellum and was, on the whole, in excellent condition. John Nicholas wondered how the book should be treated—should it be left alone or fixed up? Frank Ellis, the dealer through whom the volume was acquired, recommended that restoration be kept to a minimum—a few pages could be mended and a case should be constructed for protection. The Boccaccio arrived in Providence in the fall of 1886, and after some consideration, Brown sent the book to Paris where it was rebound by Cuzin in black morocco, as shown here.

TITLE ILLUSTRATED

Giovanni Boccaccio, *La ruine des nobles hommes et femmes*, Bruges, 1476. (fig. II.11)

II.11
Boccaccio, *La ruine des nobles hommes et femmes* (1476),
bound for John Nicholas Brown by F. Cuzin.
Height: 15.5 inches.

II.12

Invoice: F. Cuzin to John Nicholas Brown (October 18, 1887).

PART III:
Restoration

The books essential to John Carter Brown's collection of ideas were not, for the most part, the same volumes sought by European buyers in the "great books" tradition. Although they were certainly already rare in the nineteenth century, these books of American interest contained the practical accounts and discourses which had little history of collectibility as objects. Having been used rather than merely collected and protected, their condition was often worn—pages were missing or stained or mutilated. Additionally, bibliographic control of the material at that time was minimal. Without printed library records and bibliographies, ordinary tools today, assessment of certain elements of the book as an object—how many pages should it have, how many illustrations or maps, and what was an acceptable standard of condition—depended solely on the personal experience of booksellers and collectors in the field. For the John Carter Brown collection, the end result of acquiring such truly "used" books was that many volumes came to the Library in need of repair.

PEN AND INK FACSIMILES

Paid artist for time in searching for the particulars
of this rare if not unique volume . . . . £ 1.1.0

To restoring in facsimile deficiencies in the front margins
and other portions of the volume . . . . £ 2.2.0

To making facsimile title very elaborate both sides of the
page as per agreement £10.0.0

(Francis Bedford to estate of John Carter Brown, May 10, 1875)

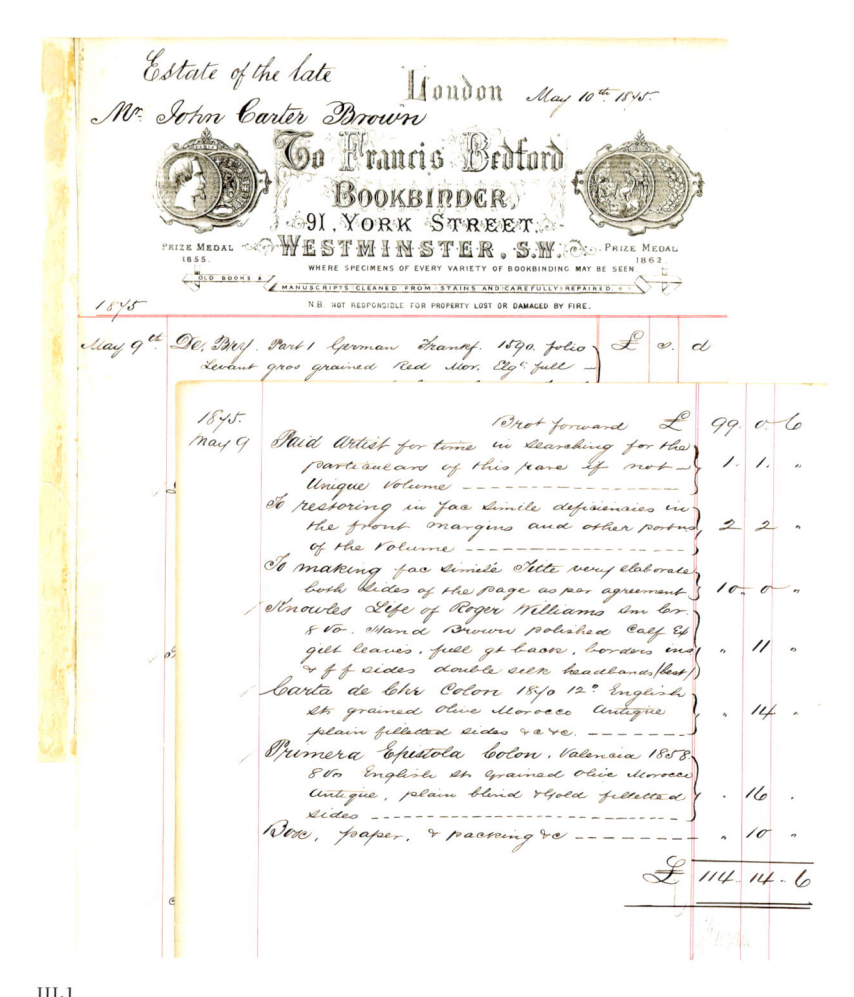

III.1
Invoice: *Francis Bedford to the estate of John Carter Brown* (May 10, 1875).

Title Page

Francis Bedford's restoration of the *Breve compendio* was extensive. The title page (an artist's pen and ink facsimile) and the repair of the paper and lost text along the right edge of the second leaf are truly remarkable. The binder's bill states that paper restoration alone required ninety-seven hours of work.

TITLE ILLUSTRATED

Martín Cortés, *Breve compendio de la sphera,* [Seville, 1551]. (fig. III.2)

III.2
Red and black pen and ink facsimile title page, Cortés, *Breve compendio* (1551).
Height: 10.5 inches.

Missing Leaves

"I would not on any account send out a book with a facsimile leaf without pointing it out, for as you say they are now sometimes so cleverly done as hardly to be recognizable."

—Frank Ellis to John Nicholas Brown, February 7, 1881.

This scarce volume, presented to the Library in 1929 by John Nicholas Brown (1900–1979), contains a facsimile leaf (the page on the right). A more complete copy has not yet been found for a "trade up." The passage above, in a letter from the bookseller Frank Ellis to John Nicholas Brown (1861–1900), points out one of the problems caused by excellent facsimile restorations.

TITLE ILLUSTRATED

Alvar Nuñez Cabeza de Vaca, *La relacion,* Zamora, [1542]. (fig. III.3)

dexaron sin que nos hiziessen ningun impedimiento
y ellos se fueron .:.

Otro dia adelante el gouernador acordo de
entrar por la tierra por descubrilla y ver lo q
enella auia. Fuymos nos cõel el comissario y
el veedor τ yo cõ qrenta hombres yentre ellos seys
de cauallo: delos quales poco nos podiamos aproue-
char. Lleuamos la via del norte hasta que a ora de bis
peras llegamos a vna vaya muy grande que a nos pare
cio que entraua mucho por la tierra. quedamos alli a
quella noche: y otro dia nos boluimos donde los nauios y gẽte estauã. El gouernador mãdo q̃ el vergãtin
fuesse costeãdo la via dela florida τ buscasse el puerto
q̃ Miruelo el piloto auia dicho q̃ sabia: mas ya el lo auia
errado y no sabia en que parte estauamos ni a dõde
era el puerto: y fue le mandado al vergantin que sino
lo hallasse traueffasse ala Hauana τ buscasse el nauio q̃
Aluaro dela çerda tenia: y tomados algunos bastimẽ
tos nos viniessen a buscar. Partido el vergantin tor-
namos a entrar enla tierra los mismos que primero
cõ alguna gente mas: y costeamos la vaya que auiamos hallado, y andadas quatro leguas tomamos
quatro indios: y mostramos les Maiz para ver si lo co
noscian porque hasta estonces no auiamos visto señal
del. Ellos nos dixero que nos lleuarian donde lo auia
Y assi nos lleuaron a su pueblo q̃ es al cabo dela baya
cerca de alli: y enel nos mostraron vn poco de maiz q̃
avn no estaua para coger se. Alli hallamos muchas ca

xas de mercaderes de Castilla: y en cada vna dellas
estaua vn cuerpo de hombre muerto: y los cuerpos
cubiertos con vnos cueros de venados pintados.
Al comissario le parescio que esto era especie de ydo-
latria: τ quemo las caxas con los cuerpos. Hallamos
tambien pedaços de lienço de paño y penachos que
parescian ser de la nueua españa. Hallamos tambien
muestras de oro. Por señas preguntamos alos indios
de adonde auian auido aquellas cosas. Señalaron
nos que muy lexos de alli auia vna prouincia que se de
zia Apalachen: enla qual auia mucho oro: y hazian se
ña de auer muy grã cantidad detodo lo que nosotros
estimamos en algo. Dezian que en Palachen auia mu
cho. Y tomando aquellos indios por guia: partimos
de alli: y andadas diez o doze leguas hallamos otro
pueblo de quinze casas donde auia buen pedaço de
Maiz sembrado que ya estaua para cogerse: y tambiẽ
hallamos alguno que estaua seco. Y despues de dos
dias que alli estuuimos nos boluimos donde el con-
tador y la gente y nauios estauan, y contamos al con
tador y pilotos lo que auiamos visto y las nueuas que
los indios nos auian dado. Y otro dia que fue primero de mayo el gouernador llamo a parte al comissario
y al cõtador y al veedor y ami y a vn marinero que se
llamaua Bartolome fernandez, y a vn escriuano que
se dezia Jeronymo de alaniz: y assi juntos nos dixo q̃
tenia en voluntad de entrar por la tierra a dentro, y
los nauios se fuessen costeando hasta que llegassen al
puerto: τ que los pilotos dezian y creyan que yendo

III.3
Nuñez Cabeza de Vaca, *La relacion* (1542). The page on the right is a pen and ink facsimile.
Height: 8.5 inches.

PAPER REPAIR

Inc. Mather Right way to shake off a Viper. 12 mo.
Boston 1710. ditto, ditto, ditto, the whole dry cl[eane]d
& the whole cl[eane]d from Ink or brown foxy spots........ £ 2.2.0

To restoring in facsimile deficient portions of title &
other portions (Inclusive)................................ − − −

Inc. Mather Wo to Drunkards Boston 1712. 12 mo.
ditto, ditto, ditto the whole dry cl[eane]d the
whole cl[eane]d from ugly brown foxy spots...
To restoring in facsimile title & other portions .... £ 2.5.0

(Francis Bedford to Sophia Augusta Brown, October 13, 1879)

It was seldom possible to acquire Mather sermons in good condition. Most of this material, so important for the study of seventeenth- and eighteenth-century American religious and moral thought, required considerable investment in preservation. The title pages of both these books have seen heavy restoration. A close look reveals repairs of paper loss, and pen and ink fill-ins of lost text. Bedford's descriptive bill for a shipment of Mather volumes is illustrative of routine repair procedures.

TITLES ILLUSTRATED

Increase Mather, *The right way to shake off a viper*, Boston, 1720. Note that paper replacement begins at the upper right corner and continues down the right side and the bottom edge. In the imprint, "Boston, N. E." is pen and ink facsimile. (fig. III.5)

Increase Mather, *Wo to drunkards*, Boston, 1712. The paper on the top and right side of the title page has been repaired and replaced. The "D. D." after "Increase Mather," is pen and ink facsimile. (fig. III.6)

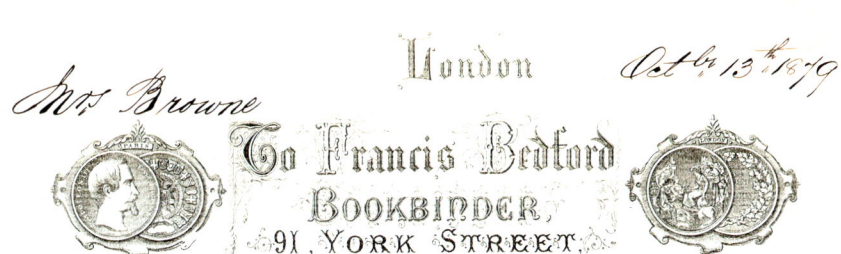

III.4
Invoice: *Francis Bedford to Sophia Augusta Brown* (October 13, 1879).

The Right Way to Shake off a Viper

AN ESSAY,

UPON A

CASE

Too commonly calling for Consideration.

What shall Good Men do, when they are Evil Spoken of?

With a Preface of
Dr. INCREASE MATHER.

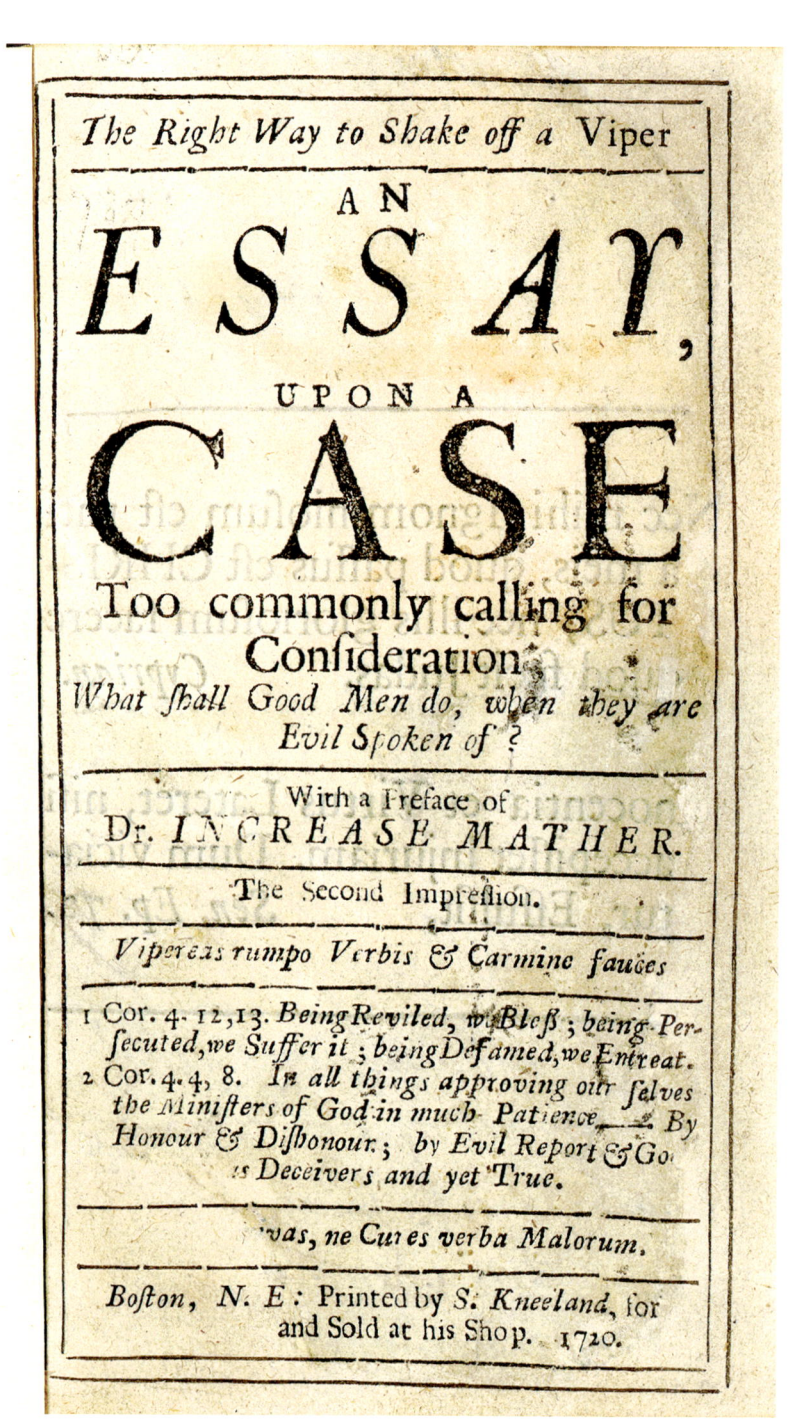

The Second Impression.

Vipereas rumpo Verbis & Carmine fauces

1 Cor. 4. 12, 13. *Being Reviled, w. Bleß ; being Persecuted, we Suffer it ; being Defamed, we Entreat.*
2 Cor. 4. 4, 8. *In all things approving our selves the Ministers of God in much Patience — By Honour & Dishonour. ; by Evil Report & Go... ... Deceivers and yet True.*

...vas, ne Cures verba Malorum.

Boston, N. E: Printed by S. Kneeland, for and Sold at his Shop. 1720.

III.5
Repaired title page, Increase Mather, *The right way to shake off a viper* (1720).
Height: 6.25 inches.

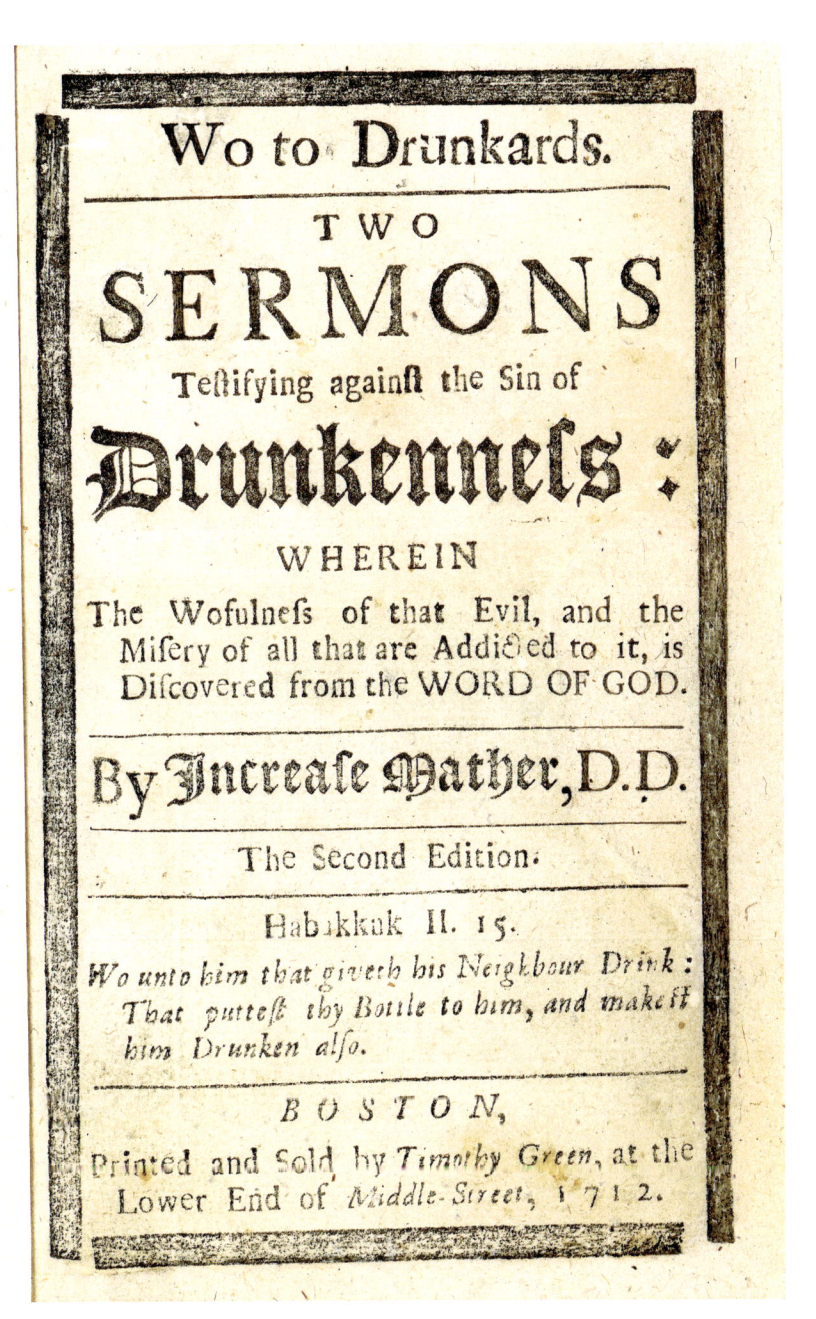

III.6
Repaired title page, Increase Mather, *Wo to Drunkards* (1712).
Height: 5.75 inches.

TRADING UP

When last in Europe I spoke to you of a copy of Hakluyt's Virginia Richly Valued of 1609. It is bound by F. Bedford, a very good copy except that pp. 67–70 (2 leaves) are in most admirable facsimile. Can you make me any good offer for this book?

—John Nicholas Brown to Henry N. Stevens, February 3, 1890

"Respecting your copy of Virginia Richly Valued 1609 (2 leaves in facsimile) I notice that perfect copies have sold in modern times for from £30 to £50. The facsimile leaves make a great difference in the price of a book and they are much more difficult to sell as collectors of this class of book prefer to wait till they get a perfect copy. Still it is a very rare book and I should be willing to allow £15 for it in exchange and trust that you will consider that a reasonable offer."

—Henry N. Stevens to John Nicholas Brown, February 14, 1890

In 1883 John Russell Bartlett sent the Brown copy of *Virginia Richly Valued* to London for rebinding. During the process, it was discovered that the book was missing two leaves. After some correspondence, it was decided to have the missing pages copied in facsimile. When a perfect replacement could be found, Brown would "trade up" and sell his imperfect volume. A few years later, a perfect copy, shown here, was acquired at auction. The correspondence between Brown and the bookseller Henry N. Stevens emphasizes the negative effect of facsimile leaves on the value of a rare book.

TITLE ILLUSTRATED

Virginia richly valued, London, 1609. (fig. III.7)

VIRGINIA
richly valued,

By the description of the maine land of Florida, her next neighbour:

Out of the foure yeeres continuall trauell and discouerie, for aboue one thousand miles East and West, of *Don Ferdinando de Soto*, and sixe hundred able men in his companie.

Wherin are truly obserued the riches and fertilitie of those parts, abounding with things necessarie, pleasant, and profitable for the life of man: with the natures and dispositions of the Inhabitants.

Written by a Portugall gentleman of *Eluas*, emploied in all the action, and translated out of Portugese by RICHARD HAKLVYT.

AT LONDON
Printed by FELIX KYNGSTON for *Matthew Lownes*, and are to be sold at the signe of the Bishops head in Pauls Churchyard.
1609.

III.7
Title page of *Virginia richly valued* (1609).
Height: 9 inches.

SOPHISTICATION

In the book world, sophistication is defined as the process through which sections of various damaged or incomplete copies of a particular edition of a book are combined to make a single volume that is bibliographically complete. These days the practice is frowned upon, but in the nineteenth century it was more acceptable, understood by dealers and collectors alike. This is not to imply that collectors lacked an appreciation of original condition. Outside the field of Americana, for instance, John Nicholas Brown was determined to acquire only perfect books, and he regularly rejected copies that had been too often through the hands of the binder and restorer. It was unrealistic, however, for collectors to expect to achieve the same standards of condition for books of American interest. When these titles appeared in nineteenth-century London bookshops and auction rooms, it was apparent that previous owners had seldom treated them as precious possessions.

Tall and Short

In this volume, evidence of sophistication is plain to the eye. Of the two copies used, one was large and relatively clean while the other was cropped and stained. Note that on the left side the restorer had to clean and extend the short page to match the tall copy.

TITLE ILLUSTRATED

Spain. [Laws, etc.], *Leyes y ordenanças nuevame[n]te hechas por Su Magestad*, Alcala de Henares, 1543. (fig. III.8)

III.8.
Spain, *Leyes y ordenancas* (1543), showing paper repairs to top of left-hand page.
Height: 12 inches.

Sophistication Incomplete

Over the years, John Carter Brown, Sophia Augusta Brown, John Russell Bartlett, Rush Hawkins, and John Nicholas Brown had all tried to complete this imperfect Mexican volume. In 1883 John Russell Bartlett suggested that it be bound, though still imperfect. It was then cleaned and inexpensively bound. Later, another copy was acquired that had some, but not all, of the missing leaves. The two imperfect copies sit side by side on the shelf still awaiting completion.

TITLE ILLUSTRATED

Fray Juan Bautista, *[Huehuetlahtolli, platicas morales de los Indios]*, Mexico, 1601. (fig. III.9)

III.9
Imperfect copies of *Huehuetlahtolli* (1601).
Heights: 8.5 inches.

More Is More

I have unpacked a box of books that came from you & I find a 4th Part of Thévenot with many titles & variations. This was intended to aid in making up your copy, the duplicates only to come back to me. I will send it (again) to you tomorrow & when you have culled it over, you may return the duplicates—I think there are some leaves which even Mr. Lenox has not."

—Henry N. Stevens to John Carter Brown, April 7, 1869

The different editions and issues of Thévenot's *Relations* are highly collectible Americana, and acquisition of the many variants was a challenge few serious collectors could ignore. This sophisticated copy, for example, contains not only the 1696 title page, shown, but also contains title pages from the editions of 1663, 1666, and 1672 that have been tipped in one right after the other.

TITLE ILLUSTRATED

Melchisédec Thévenot, *Relations de divers voyages curieux*, Paris, 1663. (fig. III.10)

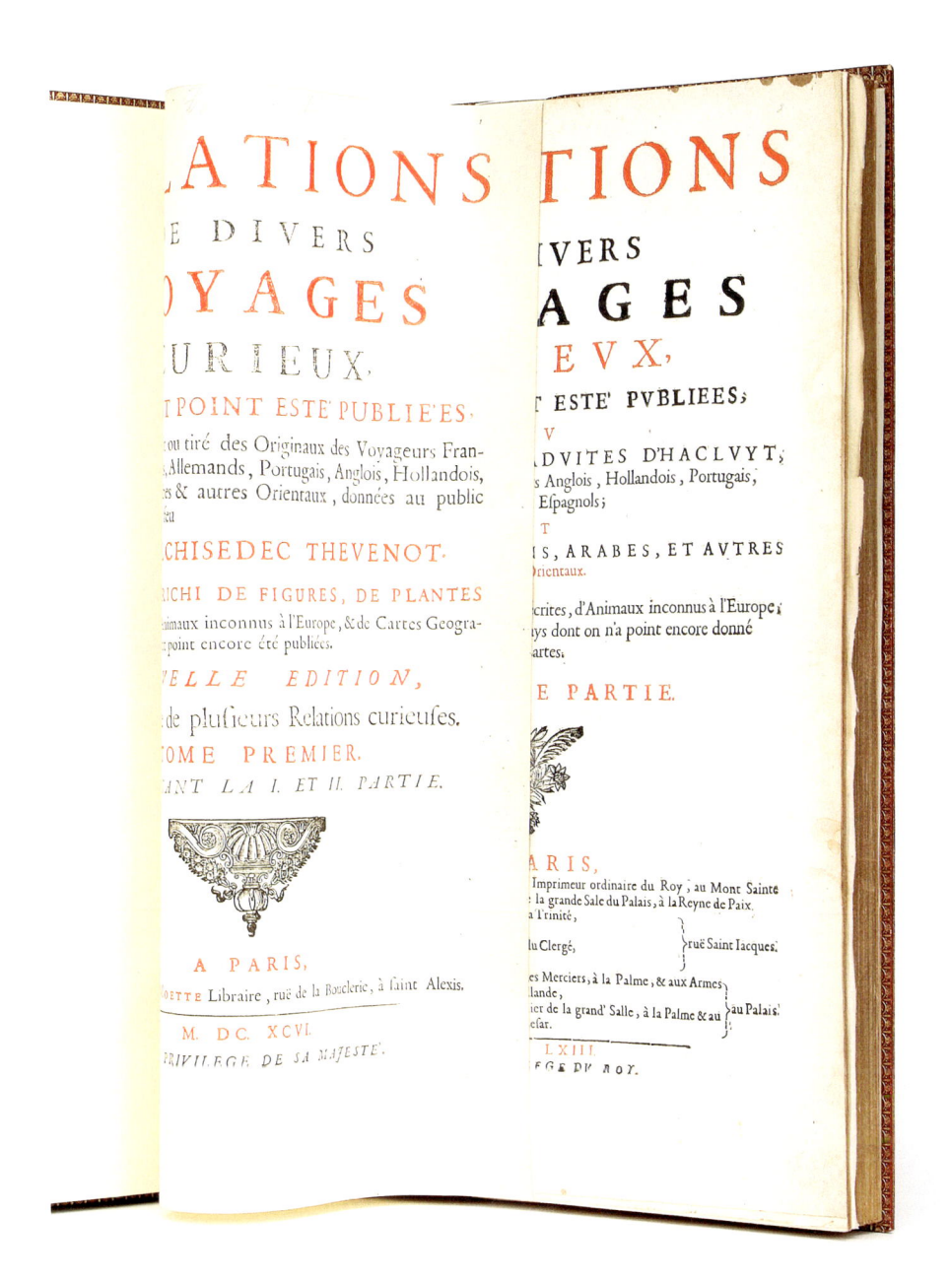

III.10

Thévenot's *Relations* (1663), showing two of the four variant title pages.
Height: 16.5 inches.

"I THINK IT BEST NOT TO TAMPER WITH IT"

I have just come across an imperfect copy of Smith's True Travels and send it to you today. You are quite welcome to exchange any leaves from this out of the Royal copy I recently sold you if found desirable to do so on comparation. You will remember that one leaf [of the Royal copy] was mended in margin. When done with please do me the favour to return this imperfect copy and the changed leaves from the Royal copy, as they will no doubt come in useful one day. Of course you will understand I make no charge for this."
—Henry N. Stevens to John Nicholas Brown, March 17, 1893

"I thank you very much for sending me the imperfect copy of Smith's True Travels and for your offer to allow me to take out any leaves that I wish and put them in my Royal copy of the same work. I will not avail myself of your offer because I prefer to keep this book as much as possible in its original state and I think it best not to tamper with it."
—John Nicholas Brown to Henry N. Stevens, April 1, 1893

While volumes were often upgraded or perfected through sophistication, there was a growing awareness during the closing years of the nineteenth century that this course of action was not always the proper one.

TITLE ILLUSTRATED

John Smith. *The true travels, adventures, and observations of Captaine Iohn Smith,* London, 1630. Original binding from the royal library of Charles II. (fig. III.11)

III.11
Smith's *True travels* (1630), with original binding of the library of Charles II.
Height: 11.5 inches.

PART IV:
Replication

FACSIMILE EDITIONS

As has been suggested, identification of facsimiles (and forgeries) is often not a simple matter. Fortunately, some present themselves in a straightforward manner. In 1868, John Carter Brown privately published this edition of his copy of Settle's account of Frobisher's voyage, which he then distributed to fellow collectors, friends, and scholars. Brown's original has closely trimmed pages; the facsimile shows what the page might have looked like before it was cropped by a succession of binders. In the nineteenth century the term "facsimile" did not necessarily mean an exact reproduction of the original image, as can be noted here.

TITLES ILLUSTRATED

Dionyse Settle, A *true report of the late voyage into the West and Northwest regions*, London, 1577. (fig. IV.1)

Dionysc Scttlc, A *true report of the late voyage into the West and Northwest regions*, London, 1577. Facsimile edition printed for John Carter Brown in 1868. (fig. IV.2)

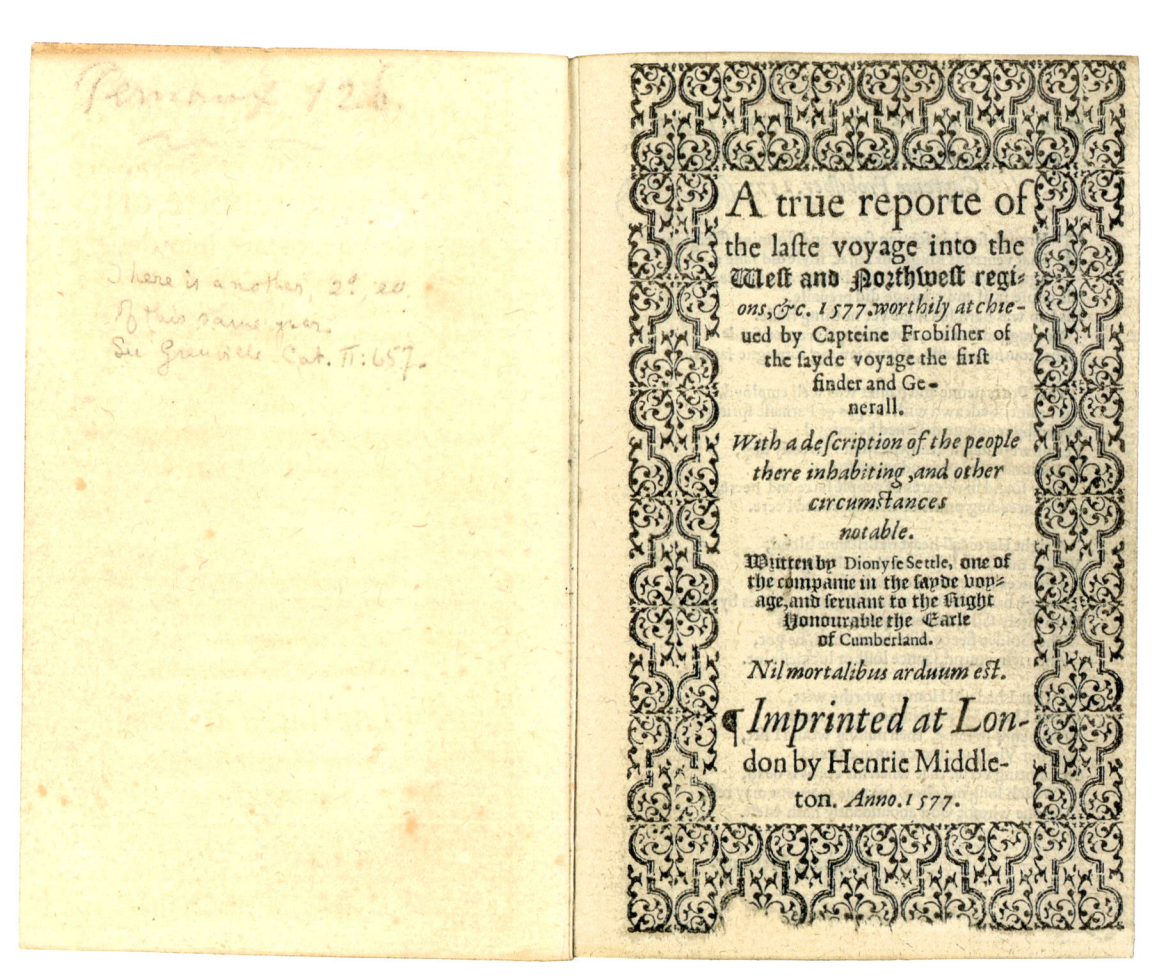

IV.1
Title page of Dionyse Settle, *A true report of the late voyage into the West and Northwest regions* (1577).
Height: 5.25 inches.

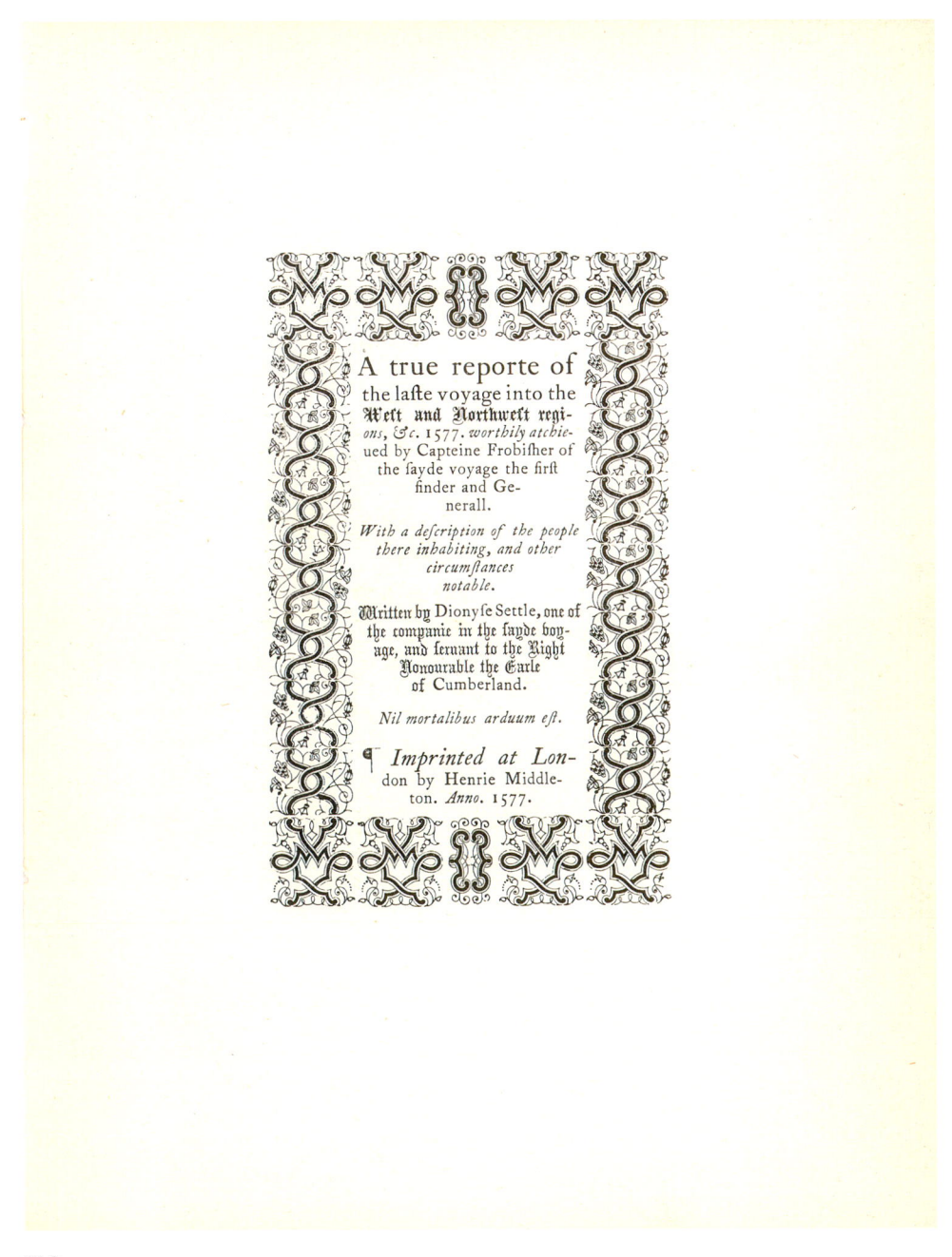

IV.2
Title page of facsimile edition of Dionyse Settle, *A true report of the late voyage into the West and Northwest regions,* printed for John Carter Brown in 1868, in fifty copies only. Height: 9 inches.

PEN AND INK FACSIMILES

Columbus Letters

He [John Nicholas Brown] says that you state that 5 copies [of the Paris Columbus Letter] are known, but he only knows of 3, viz: the two in the Bodleian & one in the University Library Gottingen.... He desires us to ask whether you have included in the 5 the copy in the Library of the late Mr. John Carter Brown of Providence, because he says that that copy is only a clever facsimile which deceived the compilers of the catalogue.... Presumably it is one of the 5 facsimiles made by Harris.

—Henry N. Stevens to E. B. Nicholson, July 4, 1893

"Columbus letters," the small printed books through which the discovery of the New World was announced to Europe, have always been highly collectible and were fitting subjects for both the facsimile artist's and the forger's art. The Letter was first published in Spanish in the spring of 1493. Before 1498, eight issues and editions had been published in Latin and two more in German and Spanish. It often requires a highly trained eye to distinguish between the genuine and the copy, and sometimes characteristics that signal a copy become apparent only when it is closely compared with a piece known to be genuine.

John Harris, Facsimile Artist

John Harris was a talented facsimile artist who worked for book dealers, collectors, and binders in London. He did not always sign his work, however, and the high quality of his facsimiles created the potential for confusion, as shown in the letter from Henry N. Stevens to E. B. Nicholson, librarian of the Bodleian Library. Shown here, side-by-side, are the originals of two Columbus Letters and the pen and ink Harris facsimiles referred to by Stevens. Harris made only five facsimiles of each of these editions and did not sign them.

TITLES ILLUSTRATED

Christopher Columbus, *Epistola*, Paris [1493]. (fig. IV.3)

Christopher Columbus, *Epistola*, Paris [1493]. Facsimile. (fig. IV.4)

"A general map, made onelye[sic] for the particuler[sic] declaration of this discovery" in Humphrey Gilbert, A *Discourse of a Discoverie for a new Passage to Cataia,* London, 1576. (fig. IV.5)

Christopher Columbus, *Epistola*, Strasbourg, 1497. (fig. IV.6)

Christopher Columbus, *Epistola*, Strasbourg, 1497. Facsimile. (fig. IV.7)

IV.3
Columbus, *Epistola* (1493).
Height: 7.5 inches.

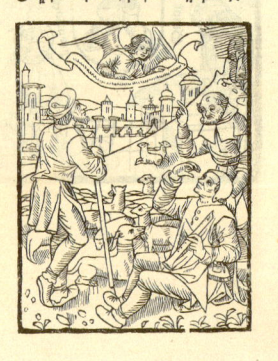

IV.4
Facsimile of Columbus, *Epistola* (1493).
Height: 7.25 inches.

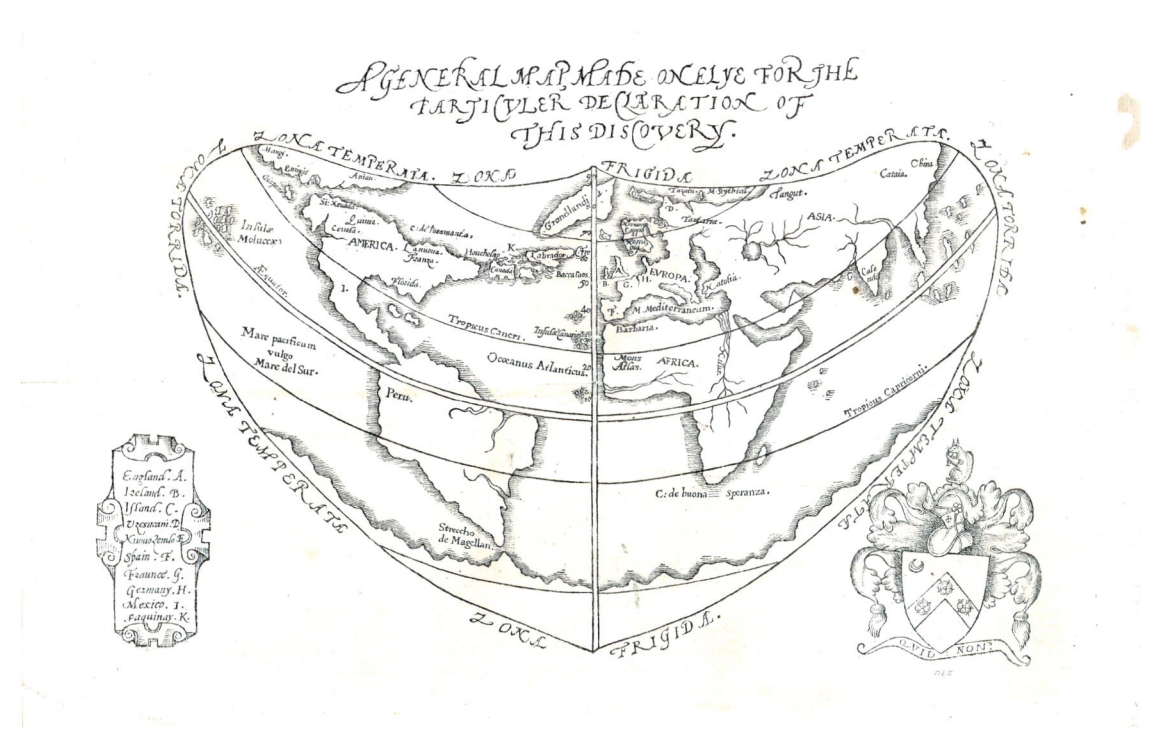

IV.5
John Harris's pen and ink facsimile of "A general map, made onelye[sic] for the particuler[sic] declaration of this discovery," in Humphrey Gilbert, *Discourse* (1576). Harris did sign this map, which he made to complete Brown's copy of Gilbert's Discourse of 1576. His initials can be detected at the lower right.
Dimensions: 8.75 × 13.5 inches.

Er houptman der schiffung des mörs Cristoferus colon von hispania schribt dem künig von hispania võ
den inßlen des lands Indie vff dem fluß gangen genant. der do flüsset am mitten durch das lande india
in das indisch mör. Die er nelichen erfunden hat. vñ
die zů finden geschickt ist mit hilff vñ groser schiffung. Und
ouch etlich vorsagung võ den inßlen. Des großmechtigisten
künigs Fernãdo genant von hispania. Nach dem vnnd ich
gefaren bin von dem gestadt des lands von hispania. das man
nennet Colũnas hercules. oder von end der welt. bin ich gefaren in dry vnd dryssig tagen in das indisch mör. Do hab ich gefunden vil inßlen mit onzalber volcks wõhafftig. Die hab ich
all ingenõmen mit vff geworffnem baner vnsers mechtigisten
künigs. Und nyeman hat sich gewidert noch darwider gestelt
in keinerley weg.   Die erst die ich gefundẽ hab/ habe ich geheissen diui saluatoris. Das ist zů tüetsch des götlichen behalters vñ selig machers. zů einer gedechtnyß syner wunderlicher
hohen maiestat die mir dar zů geholffen hat. vñ die von India
heissent sie gwanahim   Die ander hab ich geheissen vnß frowen enpfengnyß.   Uñ die dryt hab ich geheissen fernandina
nach des künigs namen. Die vierde hab ich geheissen die Hübsche insel.   Die fünffte iohãnam. vnd hab also einer yeglich-
en yren namen gegeben. Und als bald ich kam in die inßel iohannam also genant do für ich an dem gestade hinuff gegen occident wertz/ da fand ich die insel lang vnnd kein ende dar an.
Das ich gedacht es wer ein gantz land. vñ wer die prouintz zů
Cathei genant. Do sahe ich ouch keine stett noch schlõsser am
gestade des mõres. on etliche buren hüser fürst vnnd gestedel
vnd des selben glichen. Und mit den selben ynwonern mocht

a ij

iv.6
Columbus, *Epistola* (1497)
Height: 7.5 inches.

Er houptman der schiffung des mörs Cristoferus colon von hispania schribt dem künig von hispania võ den inßlen des lands Indie vff dem fluß gangen genant.der do flüsset am mitten durch das lande india in das indisch mör. Die er nelichen erfunden hat, vñ die zů finden geschickt ist mit hilff vñ groser schiffung. Und ouch etlich vorsagung võ den inßlen. Des großmechtigisten künigs Fernãdo genant von hispania. Nach dem vnnd ich gefaren bin von dem gestadt des lands von hispania, das man nennet Colũnas hercules, oder von end der welt, bin ich gefaren in dry vnd dryssig tagen in das indisch mör. Do hab ich gefunden vil inßlen mit onzalber volcks wõhafftig. Die hab ich all ingenõmen mit vff geworffnem baner vnsers mechtigisten künigs. Und nyeman hat sich gewidert noch darwider gestelt in keinerley weg. Die erst die ich gefundẽ hab/ habe ich geheissen diui saluatoris. Das ist zů tüetsch des götlichen behalters vñ selig machers, zů einer gedechtnyß syner wunderlicher hohen maiestat die mir dar zů geholffen hat, vñ die von India heissent sie gwanahim. Die ander hab ich geheissen vnß frowen enpfengnyß. Uñ die dryt hab ich geheissen fernandinã nach des künigs namen. Die vierde hab ich geheissen die hübsche insel. Die fünffte iohãnam, vnd hab also einer yeglichen yren namen gegeben. Und als bald ich kam in die inßel iohannam also genant do für ich an dem gestade hinuff gegen occident wertz / da fand ich die insel lang vnnd kein ende dar an. Das ich gedacht es wer ein gantz land, vñ wer die prouintz zů Cathei genant. Do sahe ich ouch keine stett noch schlösser am gestade des mõres, on etliche buren hüser fürst vnnd gestedel vnd des selben glichen. Und mit den selben ynwonern mocht

a ij

THE USUAL SITUATION, REVERSED

THE PENCIL NOTE on the preliminary leaf states that this German edition of Vespucci was, for many years, thought to be a facsimile. Careful examination by the bibliographer Wilberforce Eames established it as genuine, which "L. C. W.," Lawrence Wroth, JCB Librarian between 1923 and 1957, took note of.

TITLE ILLUSTRATED

Amerigo Vespucci, *Von der neu gefunden Region*, [Basel, 1505]. (fig. IV.8)

IV.8
Enlarged detail

iv.8
Vespucci, *Von der neu gefunden Region* (1505).
Height: 7.75 inches.

PART V:
Collecting the Voyages of Theodor de Bry

The travel narratives published by Theodor de Bry, sixteenth-century *National Geographic*s of sorts, were an early attempt to present the European public with an overview of the discoveries taking place on the fringes of the "civilized world." Henry Stevens of Vermont, perhaps the most colorful figure in mid-nineteenth century book collecting circles, spent a great deal of time and effort "making up" sets of de Bry's *Voyages* for his wealthy American customers. Sets of this work found in the Newberry Library, the New York Public Library, and the John Carter Brown Library were assembled, in large part, by Henry Stevens.

LARGE AND SMALL

The common division of these works into the "Great Voyages" and the "Small Voyages" has nothing to do with the importance of the particular account. The format of the "Great Voyages" is simply larger than that of the "Small Voyages."

TITLES ILLUSTRATED

Theodor de Bry, *Grands Voyages*, Part 1, English, Frankfurt, 1590. (fig. v.1)

Theodor de Bry, *Petits Voyages*, Part 1, German, Frankfurt, 1597. (fig. v.1)

v.1
Size comparison of de Bry's "Grands" and "Petits" voyages.
Dimensions: 13.75 × 10 inches and 12 × 8 inches respectively.

"ENDLESS" VARIATION

I believe that our friend Stevens imagines editions and that he pays overmuch attention to the variations occasioned by typographical errors or caprices and blunders of the binder.
—Serge Sobolewski to John Carter Brown, December 12, 1868.
Translated from the French

THE JOHN CARTER BROWN LIBRARY has nearly one hundred identically bound volumes of editions, issues, and variants of de Bry's *Voyages*. Not everyone, however, accepted Henry Stevens's pronouncements on what, exactly, was to be considered a "perfect" set, as shown by the comment from Serge Sobolewski, a noted Russian collector.

TITLES ILLUSTRATED

Theodor de Bry, *Grands Voyages*, Part 3, Latin, Frankfurt, 1592, with upside down illustration. (fig. v.2)

10 AMERICÆ

CAPVT V.

Ex Fernanbuco digreßi petimus regionem Buttugaris, sed in nauem Gallicam incidentes, prælio cum ea decertabamus.

Hinc

V.2
Upside down illustration in de Bry's *Grands voyages*. Part 3 (1592).
Height: 14 inches.

67

THE DISCUSSION CONTINUES

I have just run to earth after many years patient looking out, one of two parts of de Bry which have eluded all the great collectors of modern times.... It is the third edition of Part II Florida and is so rare that I can trace only one other copy of this variation.
—Henry N. Stevens to John Nicholas Brown, November 25, 1892

I send to you today by registered mail the part of de Bry which you sent me recently. I have not the slightest doubt as to the rarity of this book, but I do not feel like paying £105 or anything like that for a single part, which after all is a mere variation of parts, which I already have.
—John Nicholas Brown to Henry N. Stevens, December 27, 1892

Variants and editions of de Bry were still a topic of conversation a generation later, illustrated by this exchange of letters between John Carter Brown's son, John Nicholas Brown, and Henry Stevens's son, Henry Newton Stevens.

TITLE ILLUSTRATED

Theodor de Bry, *Grands voyages*, Part 2, Latin, Frankfurt, 1591, first edition. (fig. v.3)

v.3
Title page of the first edition of de Bry's *Grands voyages*, Part 2 (1591).
Height: 14 inches.

"IT WOULD STILL BE BUT AN IMITATION"

It is Part IV which wants four plates. It is very unlikely that one could meet with another coloured copy to make it up, but there would be no difficulty to find an odd part IV & take out the wanting plates & have them coloured in the same style.
—Frank Ellis to John Ncholas Brown, July 7, 1883

I have got the plates 3, 7, 9, 22, 24 to put in your coloured part IV of DeBry.... They are not coloured & I think it would not be worth while to have them done so to imitate the others, as it would still be but an imitation.
—Frank Ellis to John Nicholas Brown, October 2, 1883

M OST SETS OF de Bry's *Voyages* are "sophisticated." Indeed, the story goes that Stevens had stacks of leaves in the cellar of his shop that he collated into volumes and sets on demand. Whether or not this story is true, it is certain that there are very few volumes to be found in original condition, as issued. John Nicholas Brown had acquired several volumes of de Bry with contemporary hand-colored plates—very rare. However, some of the plates in part four were missing and the discussion in the correspondence between the London book dealer Frank Ellis and John Nicholas Brown concerns the advisability of acquiring uncolored plates, which an artist would color to match the originals.

TITLE ILLUSTRATED

Theodor de Bry, *Grands voyages*, Part 4, German, Frankfurt, 1594.
(fig. v.4)

v.4
De Bry's *Grands voyages*, Part 4 (1594), showing inserted uncolored engraving.
Height: 13 inches.

WASHING AND DRY CLEANING

The whole of the Vol dry cleaned and every leaf sized with the brush (being limp & tender) a very tiresome process & mended & map detached from clumsy thick patchings and carefully mended & lined at back with fine linen tinted to match the paper of the Vol all attended with much care & trouble soaking off patches from back margins of every leaf, the whole very troublesome. 42 hrs.
—Francis Bedford to Messrs. Rimell & Son (for John Carter Brown), August 23, 1874

In the rebinding process, paper was routinely washed, sized, and often, bleached. It was necessary to handle the contemporarily colored de Brys more carefully, and it is possible to make a tone comparison between paper washed in the routine manner and paper that has been dry-cleaned so as not to damage the color.

TITLES ILLUSTRATED

"Alligator hunt in Florida," Theodor de Bry, *Grands voyages*, Part 2, German, Frankfurt, 1591. (fig. v.6)

"Alligator hunt in Florida," Theodor de Bry, *Grands voyages*, Part 2, German, Frankfurt, 1591. (fig. v.7)

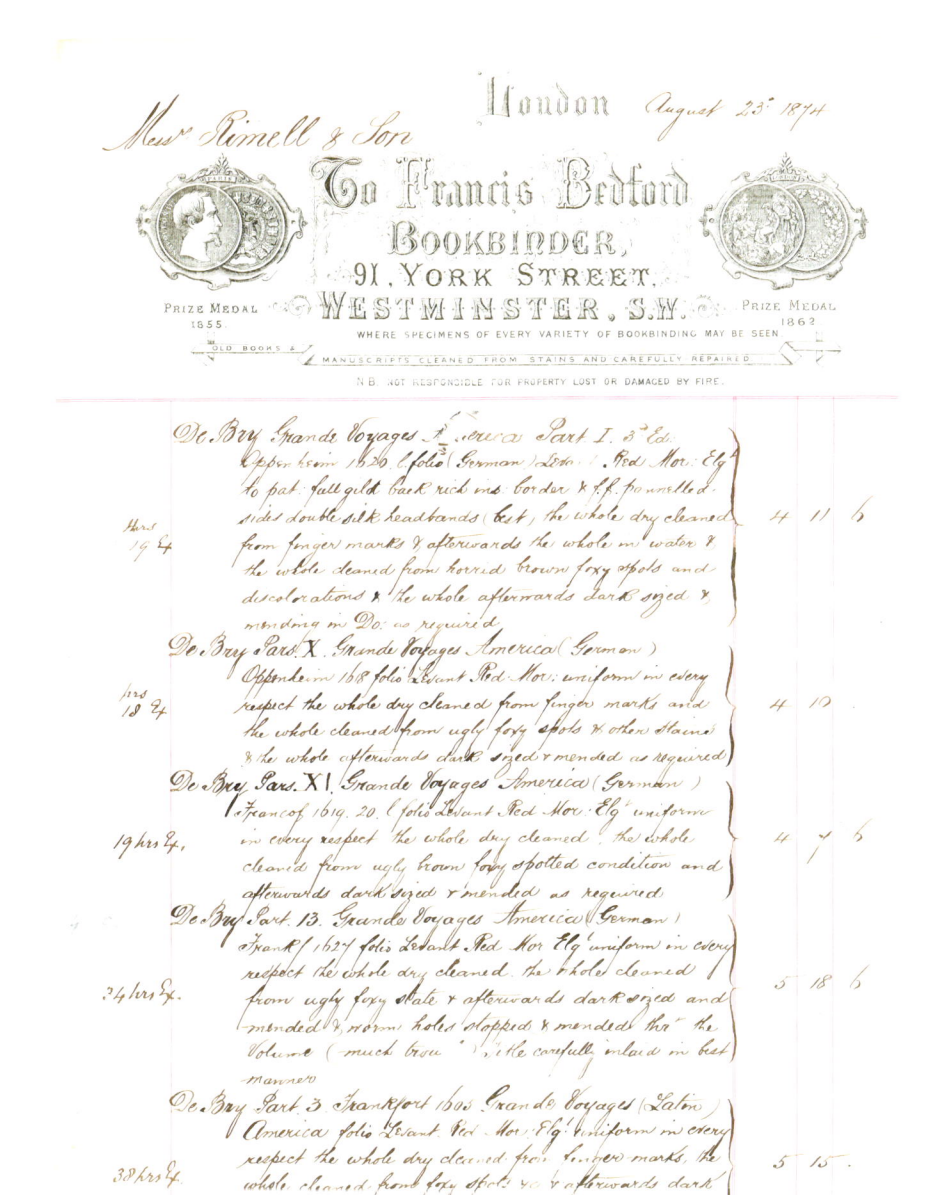

v.5
Invoice: Francis Bedford to Messrs. Rimell & Son (for John Carter Brown) (August 23, 1874). (Quotation on page 72 taken from verso.)

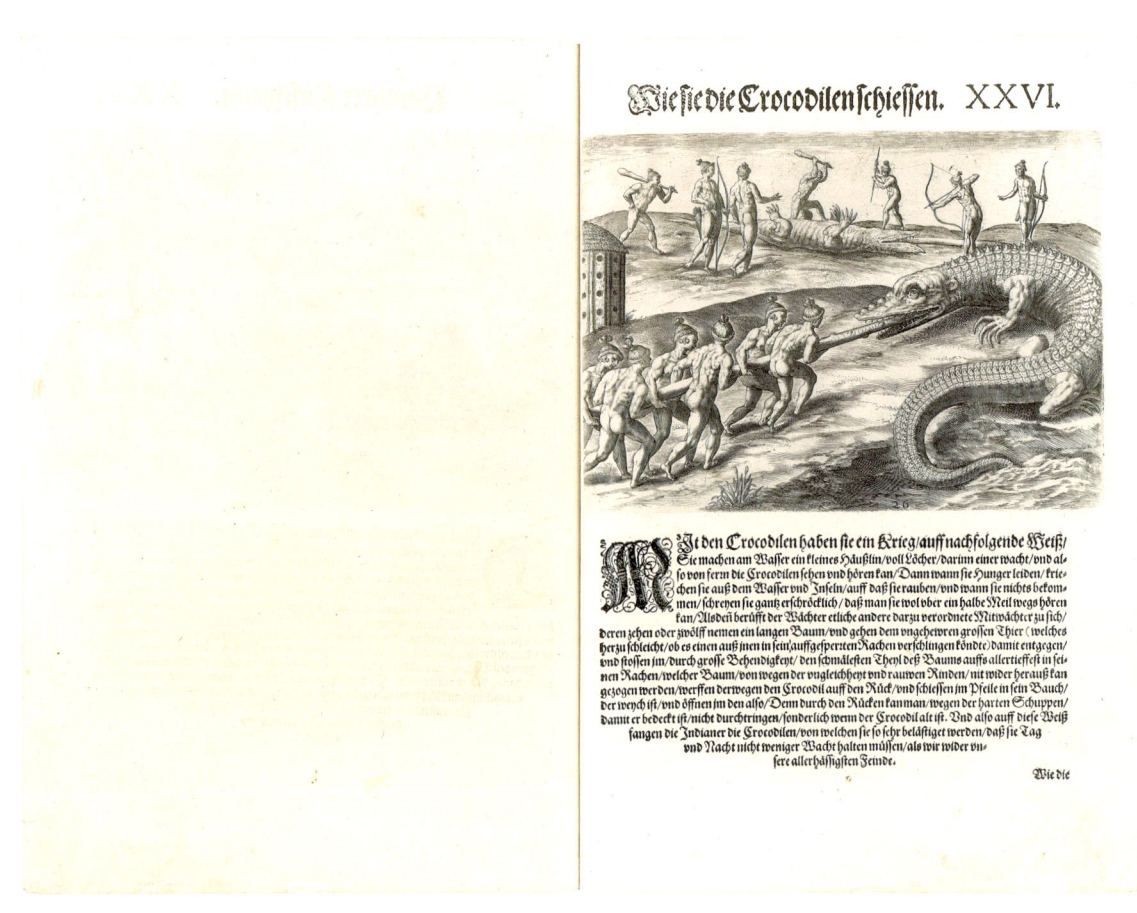

v.6
Image of the alligator hunt from de Bry's *Grands voyages*, Part 2 (1591) with washed paper.
Height: 14 inches.

v.7
Image of the alligator hunt from de Bry's *Grands voyages*, Part 2 (1591) with dry-cleaned paper.
Height: 13 inches.

PART VI:
The Aldine Press

John carter brown's early interest in the ancient classics resulted in a collection of about 325 Aldine imprints, which he amassed in the years before he began to focus on Americana. The Aldine Press, established in Venice in 1494, was one of the most distinguished printing and publishing houses in Europe during the sixteenth century. The Aldine family, particularly its founder, Aldus Pius Manutius, achieved great technical and typographical advancements with the introduction of italic type, Greek type, and the publication, for the first time, of scholarly editions of significant ancient manuscripts in a small, inexpensive format.

VI.1
Selection of books from the Aldine Press.

MAKE HASTE SLOWLY

THE TITLE PAGE device of the dolphin and anchor, representing the motto *festina lente,* proclaimed Aldus's intent—quickness and firmness in the execution of a great scheme but yet undertaken with care. The device was in continuous use by the family until the expiration of their publishing business in the third generation.

TITLE ILLUSTRATED

Lodovico Celio Ricchieri, *Sicuti antiquarum lectionum,* Venice, 1516. (fig. VI.2)

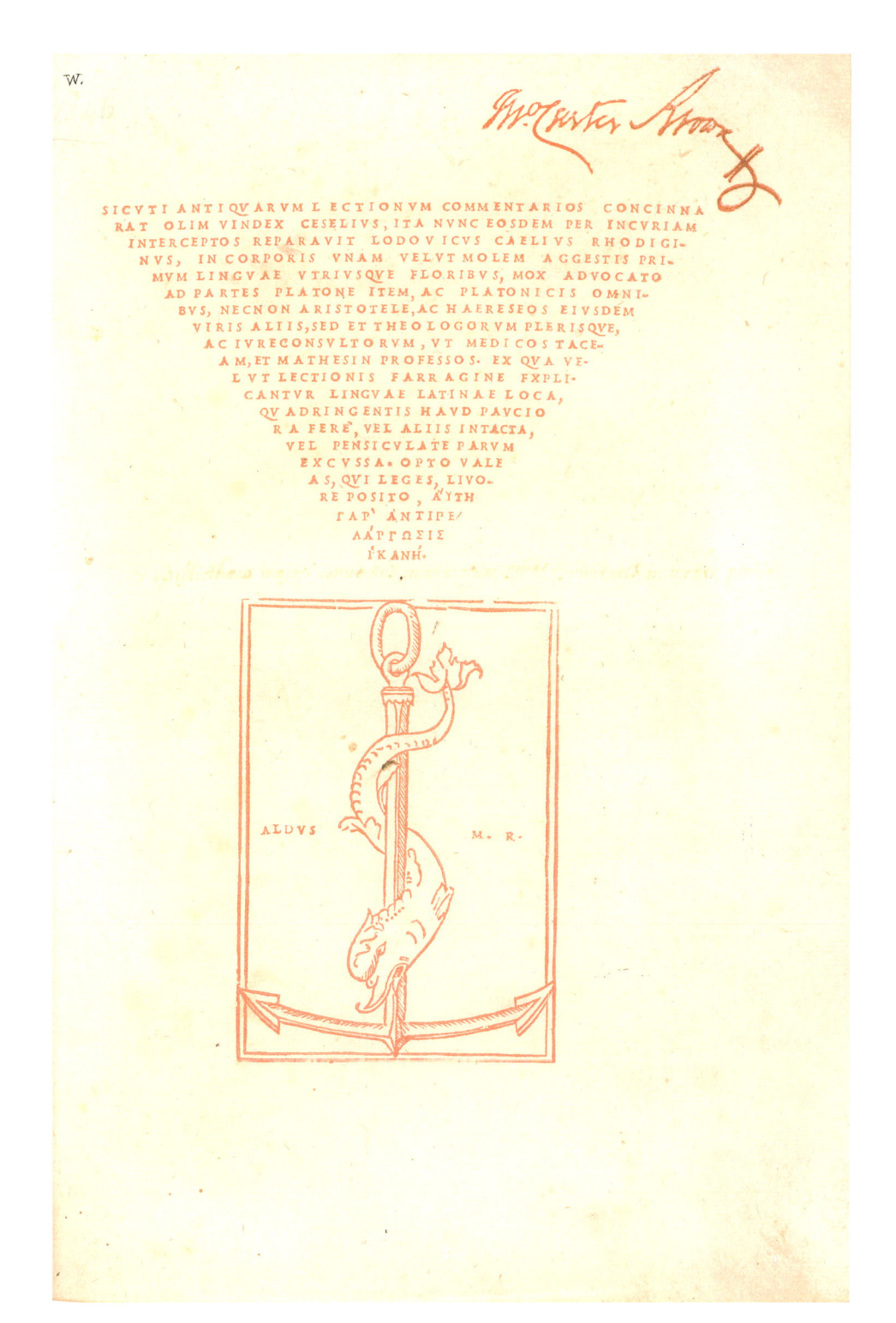

VI.2
Aldine dolphin and anchor device on title page of Ricchieri, *Sicuti antiquarum* (1516).
Height: 12 inches.

Aldine imprints captured the attention of the book buying public, and enterprising publishers in Lyons, Basel, Venice, and Toscolano reciprocated by producing a long series of counterfeits in the course of the sixteenth century. Many of these illegal editions captured the textual accuracy and physical attributes of the original Aldines and are ample proof of the rapid, positive reception accorded these innovative volumes. The book shown here has been identified as a counterfeit. One of the signs of fraud is a typographical error—the first line of the last page reads "73" instead of "75." Whoever published this piracy also copied the Aldine logo—the dolphin and anchor—from a genuine Aldine.

TITLE ILLUSTRATED

Camillo Porzio, *La congiura de' baroni del regno di Napoli*, [Rome? 1565?]. (fig. vi.3)

VI.3
Title page of the counterfeit edition, Porzio, *La congiura* (1565?).
Height: 8.75 inches.

John carter brown's personal catalogue of his Aldine collection reveals that he was unaware that counterfeit Aldine editions were among his possessions. Entry 3 for 1565 describes the Porzio *La congiura* as an authentic Aldine.

TITLE ILLUSTRATED

"Catalogue of Aldine Editions and Rare Classical Works in the Library of John Carter Brown," Providence, 1862. (fig. vi.4)

vi.4
Entry for Porzio's *La congiura* (1565?) in John Carter Brown's "Catalogue of Aldine Editions" (1862).

CREATIVE COUNTERFEITS

I do not know whether you read the London 'Athenaeum'—there was an account of an elaborately contrived forgery in it a few weeks since. His modus operandi was to manufacture a title and preface and to supply the body of the book by some worthless volume—the scoundrel presuming on the buyer not looking beyond the title for some time at least.

—Frank Ellis to John Nicholas Brown, August 15, 1885

Although the Brown family was sometimes fooled by counterfeits, they were not the only dupes among collectors. Just as the popularity of the Aldines during the sixteenth century induced other publishers to pirate Aldine book design, other collectible editions led unscrupulous dealers to be so daring as to make up facsimile titles and prefaces and to attach them to worthless texts. This communication from Frank Ellis to John Nicholas Brown (d. 1900) sheds light on the scandalous practices of a book dealer in the late nineteenth century.

PART VII:
Fore-Edge Painting

Fore-edge painting is the almost exclusively English practice of painting a water color on the fanned out fore-edge of a book. There are also double paintings–one scene revealed when the pages are fanned to the right, the second when the pages are fanned to the left. When the painting is dry the page edges are gilded or marbled so that the closed book shows no trace of the painting. Subjects depicted included portraits, country estates, ruined castles, seascapes, and landscapes. The types of books most frequently embellished were Bibles, prayer books, the classics, travel books, and poetry. The John Carter Brown Library has six books with fore-edge paintings, a practice that began in the eighteenth century. Two with seascapes are shown here.

TITLES ILLUSTRATED

The whole book of Psalms: collected into English metre by Thomas Sternhold and John Hopkins, Oxford, 1798. (fig. VII.1)

William Wilberforce, *A practical view of the prevailing religious system*, London, 1829. (fig. VII.2)

VII.1
Seascape painted on the fore-edge of *The whole book of Psalms* (1798).
Height: 8.5 inches.

VII.2
Seascape painted on the fore-edge of Wilberforce, *A practical view* (1829).
Height: 8.5 inches.

This book was designed
and set in type by Gilbert Design Associates
in Providence, Rhode Island.
The type is Bulmer, based on the types
cut by William Martin for William Bulmer's
Shakespeare Press c. 1790.
This book was printed by Reynolds DeWalt
on Scheufelen paper.
It was bound by Acme Bookbinding
in Charlestown, Massachusetts.
The stamping dies used on the covers are
copies made from the originals
at the John Carter Brown Library.

1,000 copies for
The John Carter Brown Library
May 2008